"Dr. Hemphill reveals how addiction treatment pioneered integrated care because of its unique bio-psycho-social-spiritual recovery paradigm. He illuminates the unique ways addiction treatment has been adapted to the modern medical treatments available today. By highlighting these adaptations, he identifies which techniques set addiction treatment apart, explains why these techniques are such powerful tools, and shows how to use these techniques to implement coordinated care models. Those who read this work will walk away empowered by perceiving the existing connectivity hidden within the shadows of the looming silos of our healthcare system's various specializations. Early intervention and addressing access disparities have never been more critical to healthcare services than now, and this book offers innovative solutions that any healthcare leader can utilize for optimal care."

Mark S. Gold, *MD, distinguished alumni professor chairman and emeritus eminent scholar, University of Florida & McKnight Brain Institute*

"In this timely and prescient book, Dr. Hemphill has put into actionable form the meaning of 'we're all in this together.' Addiction has crippled individuals, families, and communities for millennia, and modern approaches to addiction have come from seemingly disparate origins that include religious, medical, behavioral, and new age approaches. All of these have contributed in some way to the evolution of a more humane, compassionate, science-driven, and spiritual approach to treating addiction. Dr. Hemphill has outlined, through research and experience, his vision of how truly integrated care for individuals and families with addiction can and should unfold. As an Addiction Psychiatrist who has worked in the trenches for nearly 40 years, I believe that his map pointing to the way out of the quagmire of addiction is one that can be trusted to produce results."

Alexis Polles, *MD, medical director and CEO, Florida Professionals Resource Network*

Integrated Care in Addiction Treatment

This book emphasizes the importance of integrative care among the healthcare professionals involved in addiction treatment and includes a plan for executing and assessing the success of the system.

Drawing on three decades of experience helping practitioners, managers, administrators, and funders understand and implement this treatment, Dr. Hemphill discusses the history and integration of coordinated care, and details how it works in practice from the medical and business perspectives. He outlines a model that encourages the expansion of detection systems and stresses the importance of behavioral health treatment in addiction treatment centers, which can reduce treatment costs and enhance care management. Resources are included for assessing organizational readiness, monitoring outcomes, and suggestions for continuous improvement to ensure a seamless transition, leading to better outcomes, patient engagement, and worker job satisfaction.

This book offers innovative solutions that any healthcare professional practicing behavioral health and addiction medicine can utilize to ensure optimal care.

Philip Hemphill, PhD, has over 30 years of practical experience as a clinician, manager, professor, executive, and consultant implementing integrative care models. He has been a professor at Tulane University School of Social Work and an assistant clinical faculty at Louisiana State University Health Sciences.

Integrated Care in Addiction Treatment

Philip Hemphill

NEW YORK AND LONDON

First published 2022
by Routledge
605 Third Avenue, New York, NY 10158

and by Routledge
2 Park Square, Milton Park, Abingdon, Oxon, OX14 4RN

Routledge is an imprint of the Taylor & Francis Group, an informa business

© 2022 Philip Hemphill

The right of Philip Hemphill to be identified as the author of this work has been asserted by her in accordance with sections 77 and 78 of the Copyright, Designs and Patents Act 1988.

All rights reserved. No part of this book may be reprinted or reproduced or utilised in any form or by any electronic, mechanical, or other means, now known or hereafter invented, including photocopying and recording, or in any information storage or retrieval system, without permission in writing from the publishers.

Trademark notice: Product or corporate names may be trademarks or registered trademarks, and are used only for identification and explanation without intent to infringe.

Library of Congress Cataloging-in-Publication Data
Names: Hemphill, Philip, author.
Title: Integrated care in addiction treatment / Philip Hemphill.
Description: 1 Edition. | New York, NY : Routledge, 2022. | Includes bibliographical references and index. |
Identifiers: LCCN 2021019327 (print) | LCCN 2021019328 (ebook) | ISBN 9780367652425 (hardback) | ISBN 9780367652418 (paperback) | ISBN 9781003128571 (ebook)
Subjects: LCSH: Substance abuse--Treatment. | Addicts--Rehabilitation. | Strategic planning.
Classification: LCC HV4998 .H46 2022 (print) | LCC HV4998 (ebook) | DDC 362.29--dc23
LC record available at https://lccn.loc.gov/2021019327
LC ebook record available at https://lccn.loc.gov/2021019328

ISBN: 978-0-367-65242-5 (hbk)
ISBN: 978-0-367-65241-8 (pbk)
ISBN: 978-1-003-12857-1 (ebk)

DOI: 10.4324/9781003128571

Typeset in Times New Roman
by MPS Limited, Dehradun

Contents

Foreword		ix
Preface		xi
Acknowledgments		xv
1	The Ground Floor	1
2	History of Integrated Care and Addiction	9
3	Overcoming Barriers	27
4	Making the Ethical Case	32
5	Making the Business Case	43
6	Whole Person Care	51
7	Care Coordination & Insurance Companies	67
8	Communication	73
9	Measurement-Based Care	79
10	Patient Experience	94
11	The Role of Leadership	99

12 Coordinated Care on a Spectrum	118
13 Considerations for Different Settings	126
14 The Payoff	138
Index	141

Foreword

In *Integrated Care in Addiction Treatment* Dr. Philip Hemphill calls upon healthcare experts to lead the way in collaboratively revolutionizing our healthcare system. Upwards of 70% of diagnoses and treatment for mental health issues occur in a primary care setting. While primary care, OB-GYN, and other providers make the majority of the diagnoses, there is a disconnect after that. Only 10% of patients diagnosed with depression in this setting achieve remission. This statistic reveals that some of the basic integrated care principles are already understood, yet we are still not seeing the desired healthcare outcomes. Some of the problems are the lack of the commonly prescribed SSRI medications to work, and what primary care providers expect. The other part is the one-size-fits-all version of modern healthcare services.

Dr. Hemphill reveals how addiction treatment, out of necessity, pioneered integrated care because of its unique bio-psycho-social-spiritual recovery paradigm. Historically, the diagnosis of addiction by itself implied a lack of spiritual and emotional wellbeing. This often led to the individualization of treatment which was somewhat unique for each patient. Dr. Hemphill illuminates the unique ways the addiction treatment has been adapted to the modern medical treatments available today. By highlighting these adaptations, Dr. Hemphill identifies which techniques set addiction treatment apart, explains why these techniques are such powerful tools, and shows how to use these techniques to implement integrated care models.

The beauty of Dr. Hemphill's proposal is that the solution is simple yet profound. This is illustrated by explaining the barriers to coordinated care, namely (1) the lack of buy-in and (2) compartmentalization. In short, nearly all the tools required are currently available; it is mostly a matter of philosophical change. While such paradigm shifts are not accomplished purely by authoring a new mission statement, the path forward is within the very term "integrated care," i.e., integrating care services.

However, one major piece of the puzzle missing: Is treatment better, evidence-based, and cost-effective? With that said, one of the most convincing aspects of integrated care is its cost-effectiveness. By prioritizing the patient, integrated care increases early intervention, treats concurrent medical-dental-infectious-psychiatric and other real problems. Whole patient treatment is logical and also improves program-treatment retention. At the same time, it reduces overall healthcare costs, hospital admissions, and emergency department visits. At this point in the book that Dr. Hemphill makes perhaps the most transformational recommendation for our healthcare system: Care coordinators. By providing care coordinators, insurance companies can supply the most critical tool in implementing integrated care while increasing the insurance company's ability to accurately assess the patient's case.

Dr. Hemphill's extensive working knowledge of our healthcare system shines through in *Integrated Care in Addiction Treatment* as he offers a wealth of evidence and advice concisely, meeting all healthcare professionals where they are in their organizations. His current work offers inspiration in the form of attainability by showcasing that integrated care is fundamentally a lifestyle change for our healthcare workers. Those who read this work will walk away empowered by perceiving that the existing connectivity is hidden within the shadows of the looming silos of our healthcare system's various specializations. Early intervention and addressing access disparities have never been more critical to healthcare services than now as we all find our footing in a COVID world, and this book offers innovative solutions that any healthcare leader can utilize for optimal care.

Mark S. Gold, MD, distinguished life fellow, the American Psychiatric Association; distinguished fellow, American College of Clinical Pharmacology; distinguished fellow, American Society of Addiction Medicine; professor, Neuroscience, Psychiatry, Anesthesiology, Community Health & Family Medicine; chief, distinguished professor, eminent scholar, distinguished alumni professor, chairman and emeritus eminent scholar University of Florida & McKnight Brain Institute-retired.

Preface

As I sat down to write this book, I found myself thinking back, time and again, to the vibrant characters that colored my childhood in New Orleans. Growing up in that rich cultural stew gave me an abiding appreciation for the beauty and diversity of the human spirit and an endless fascination with the workings of the human mind.

As a young man, I often found myself wondering how so many people living so closely together and sharing a common culture could have such profoundly different experiences of life. As I came of age, I began to realize that oftentimes *joie de vivre* in the Big Easy could be anything but—that the smiling masks of Mardi Gras could hide trauma, depression, addiction, and dysfunction. I have dedicated the better part of my adult life as a researcher and practicing social worker to understand this dichotomy and identifying the best ways to help people overcome the challenges of our shared human condition.

I wrote this book in a New Orleans that no longer thought of itself as post-Katrina. It has been years since we were feverishly swapping stories of our miserable evacuation or our regretful decision to stay in town.

By the time I started writing, the 10th anniversary of that horribly destructive storm had come and gone, marked by large gatherings: Memorial services, volunteer projects, second-line parades, political marches, and block parties. Clearly, the unofficial theme was "working through our trauma together."

But, as these things go, it took a while to finish my manuscript. As I picked the draft back up to write the final pages, we were deep into the COVID-19 pandemic. On January 9, 2020, the World Health Organization speculated that a spate of pneumonia-like cases in Wuhan, China, could have stemmed from a new coronavirus (American Journal of Managed Care, 2021). And, later that month, the Centers for Disease Control & Prevention confirmed the United States' first case.

By May, over 20 million American jobs had disappeared (Soucheray, 2020). A large segment of our country began sliding into poverty, through no fault of their own. Some of the hardest-hit economic sectors—food service, bars, and hotels—were those that fuel the New Orleans economy.

xii *Preface*

A Black man in Minneapolis, Minnesota was among those who lost his job as a result of the pandemic. On May 25, George Floyd was arrested outside a store after an employee reported that he was paying for cigarettes with counterfeit money. Floyd would die in police custody. The footage of his final moments went viral. The video showed a white police officer kneeling on Floyd's neck after he had been restrained (BBC News, 2020). The nation erupted with anger over his and other cases of brutality toward black people.

A few months later, at the end of a long and lonely summer, the 15th anniversary of Hurricane Katrina arrived. This time, it was not marked with memorial services and block parties. But, just the same, the large gatherings came. This time, they were anti-mask rallies and Black Lives Matter protests.

In February 2021, as I prepared to submit a polished version of this book to my editors, New Orleans prepared for a Mardi Gras with no parades or balls. We decorated our houses more than usual. We sent each other plenty of king cakes. We celebrated, instead, the stilted rollout of two very impressive vaccines. With lockdowns and other epidemiological measures failing to curb the spread in the United States, the vaccines seemed to be our only hope.

Globally, over 3.5 million people have died from COVID-19 (Institute for Health Metrics and Evaluation, 2021). In Louisiana alone, we have lost 8,778 brothers, sisters, colleagues, and friends. Unfortunately, the pandemic has resulted in a 20% increase in fatal overdoses from opioids and other drugs in the 12-month period ending June 2020 (Stephenson, 2021).

The legacy of COVID-19 will be a different kind of trauma than Hurricane Katrina. As a behavioral health professional, the hardest thing for me to watch is all of these systemic traumas unfolding in real time—knowing the mental health impacts that people will go through in the next couple of years and the limited access to mental health services.

Our times reveal a disrupted world that continues to experience an existential crisis. Individuals, groups, communities, and societies have been forced to re-examine the meaning and value of care. Most have been forced to reconcile their conceptualization of "survival mode" with being reduced at times to a fundamental, simplistic existence that reminds me a great deal of the existence of those suffering from addiction.

The pandemic forced everyone in the world into survival mode at once. We are using all our energies just to get by. We cannot actualize or be creative or even enjoy our hobbies. We are just getting our basic needs met—if that.

In many ways, this is a book about human complexity. Addiction makes life extremely simple in some ways. All of a person's faculties are focused on obtaining a substance. But it is actually an extremely complicated illness. And it requires a similarly complex response.

While integrated approaches seem logical to many of today's clinicians, especially in the wake of COVID-19, integrated addiction treatment is a relatively new concept. As it can happen in life, being in the right places at the right times allowed me to witness the birth of integrated behavioral healthcare and to play a role in its adoption and use.

My career has allowed me to implement complex healthcare transformations to build out integrated care in a provider organization. In my perspective, all intricate processes—at least the successful ones—begin with a commitment to humility. A recognition that you do not know all the answers.

The path forward is paved with nothing less than profound self-reflection and a desire to understand all stakeholders' beliefs, experiences, values, decisions, motivations, differences, biases, honors, prior generations, commodities, time, relationships, consequences, spirituality, and more. Going through this process multiple times with different organizations has allowed me to synthesize and communicate some general principles of integrated care implementations.

This book draws greatly on my career. I draw from the professional experiences I have had and the positions I have held, through which the integration of care has flowed. At the beginning of my career, I was fortunate to be offered a position at a treatment facility where history was being made. And from then on, I have continued to enjoy opportunities to transform healthcare by integrating behavioral health into "whole person" care.

This book provides a basic framework for the implementation and use of integrated care in addiction treatment. By demonstrating the value of the approach and how current systems of care can evolve to include integrated care, I hope to speed the adoption of this approach. The global pandemic and opioid crisis are already forcing our systems of care to adopt a phased integrated approach with integrated care. This tragic year of deadly infections, deadly violence, and terrible isolation calls for integrated, coordinated systems.

Integration? Coordination? What to call this type of care? There are a lot of terms thrown about. In the weeks before I submitted the first full draft to my publisher, I continued to struggle with this. Shared language is incredibly important. Bringing behavioral and primary care together requires no less than a meeting of two fully separate cultures. We have to be able to talk to one another.

When I was trained back in the 80s, I worked a lot with people with dissociative disorders and people using their defense mechanisms to survive. Professionals would say they needed to be "integrated" into a whole person again. They needed to have all these different parts of their self come back together. From that same use, however, the term "dis-integrated" has been viewed as non-inclusive. It is the sense that, when someone has an addictive disorder there is a need to integrate all of who they are.

Another challenge with this term is the risk that it could be confused with integrative medicine, which implies the use of a mix of approaches, some of which may not be supported by peer-reviewed research. This potential is increased by the fact that I do promote a version of healthcare that incorporates spirituality and calls for cultural humility that acknowledges the shortcomings of Western medicine. But that is where the similarities end. This book is not about integrative medicine.

Ultimately, however, I stuck with the term "integrated care" because my vision of the term largely aligns with that used by SAMHSA and AHRQ: "tightly integrated, on-site teamwork with a unified care plan as a standard approach to care for designated populations. Connotes organizational integration involving social and other services" (Agency for Healthcare Research and Quality, 2013).

I also considered collaborative care, multidisciplinary care, whole care, and whole-person care. These are valid descriptions of the model and standard of care that I am promoting, so you will notice that I use them on occasion throughout the book.

I do not want to get too hung up on terminology. Language does matter. What matters so much more, however, is the patient outcomes.

As more programs follow these best practices, we can improve the level of healthcare overall—and for addiction in particular.

References

Agency for Healthcare Research and Quality. (2013, April). In C. J. Peek (Ed.), *Lexicon for behavioral health and primary care integration.* Retrieved from https://integrationacademy.ahrq.gov: https://integrationacademy.ahrq.gov/sites/default/files/2020-06/Lexicon_ExecSummary.pdf

American Journal of Managed Care. (2021, January 1). *A timeline of COVID-19 developments in 2020.* Retrieved February 21, 2021, from https://www.ajmc.com/view/a-timeline-of-covid19-developments-in-2020

BBC News. (2020, July 16). *George Floyd: What happened in the final moments of his life.* Retrieved February 21, 2021, from https://www.bbc.com/news/world-us-canada-52861726

Institute for Health Metrics and Evaluation. (2021, February 21). *COVID-19 projections.* Retrieved February 21, 2021, from https://covid19.healthdata.org: https://covid19.healthdata.org/global?view=total-deaths&tab=trend

Soucheray, S. (2020, May 8). *US job losses due to COVID-19 highest since Great Depression.* Retrieved February 21, 2021, from Center for Infectious Disease Research and Policy: https://www.cidrap.umn.edu/news-perspective/2020/05/us-job-losses-due-covid-19-highest-great-depression

Stephenson, J. (2021, January 5). *CDC warns of surge in drug overdose deaths during COVID-19.* doi:10.1001/jamahealthforum.2021.0001

Acknowledgments

This manuscript has been developed over years of practice with numerous colleagues and health systems. I have always been committed to providing best practices for individuals and their families struggling with mental health and addiction needs. These partnerships have provided a formative experience that has allowed me to generate the concepts, strategies, and recommendations expressed here. By taking a position of humility, I have acquired an amalgam of approaches to these complex needs and attempt to offer diverse solutions.

Bringing a manuscript to publication requires considerable feedback from these partners throughout my thirty-two-year career in the behavioral health and addiction industry. While it is impossible to capture everyone or every system, I have identified the key individuals and organizations throughout the book and have always been proud to represent them when actively engaged or as time has passed. They have instilled in me the importance of remaining agile and innovative. Organizations that do not evolve will dwindle.

I appreciate the Executive leaders who included me and gave me the opportunities to understand this path (the late Darryl Sue White and Vicki Pevsner, Marty Drell, Debbie Sanford, Roy Serpa, and Noah Nordheimer); the thought leaders who have encouraged me throughout my career (Mark Schwartz, Lori Galperin, Dan Glaser, Mark Gold, Alexis Polles, Charles Figley, and Jerry Vaccaro); colleagues (Ellis Lindsey, Scott Brothers, Lisa Lucas, Diane Markel, and Reggie Parquet) and others for continuously offering manuscript commentary and encouragement (Molly Kramer, Grace McDonnell, Amanda Devine, and Tanya Kapoor).

The most important partners have always been the individuals I have worked with who struggle with health conditions; their motivation and willingness to share their experiences have inspired me.

Finally, my family members who are my original learning partners. You have been patient and encouraging throughout this manuscript which represents your experiences with me. I have been inspired to be your coordinator at times, your innovator when change was inevitable, and your integrator when necessary, across all of my responsibilities.

1 The Ground Floor

All behavioral health providers learn about humanity. But those who specialize in treating professionals learn the most about human capacity. We observe the highest limits of it.

We learn what volume of stress a human can endure. We are struck by the surprising level of compassion that can be maintained over the decades of a career. We see what heights the human brain can achieve. And we observe what little support is needed to just keep a human being going as they start to burn out.

While working with healthcare providers, I thought back to the times when programming classes were taken in college. As undergraduates, we needed credits in either a foreign language or computer science. After a horrendous semester of Italian, I decided to switch to computers. In those days, that meant learning Fortran, Pascal, or BASIC. I ended up taking several languages, learning how to produce the required outcome in each.

A large percentage of a programmer's time is spent debugging the code. When a program does not produce the desired outcome, you have to go back through the code line by line to find out what is causing the "run-time error."

Dealing with complex behavioral health and addiction problems is very similar to debugging. Albeit the human brain is, of course, endlessly more complicated.

If we think of the individual as a computer with the brain as the motherboard, the mind would be the operating system. We see the output of this operating system in the behavior of the individuals, and it is either the desired or undesired output.

If it is the latter, the system needs debugging. This means digging down into the code and finding the sections that are producing the run-time errors. Just as an OS has multiple libraries and frameworks to check, the mind and body have numerous facets that contribute to mental health and addiction. In the case of humans, debugging is a multidisciplinary task. It involves many different clinicians with many different degrees, specialties, and life experiences.

Modern addiction treatment is similar to a psychoanalytic-oriented approach, but it is much broader in scope. Psychoanalysis can be reductionistic: Say a person is suffering from addiction because they are dealing with the pain of a traumatic event. That is certainly the place to begin to unravel the threads, but such myopic perspectives fail to consider the numerous complex factors and systems that contribute to behavior.

For example, is the patient even interested in reliving, revising, and resolving their trauma? What type of trauma was it? Was physical pain involved? Can medical treatment or medications address that pain? What about the emotional pain? Has it affected the person's self-image? What other factors led them to experience the trauma in that particular way? Can we address those issues? How do society's reaction and acceptance (or lack thereof) contribute? Are there cultural variations in managing these experiences or even labeling them traumatic? Would the individual's life and those around them be enhanced by resolving their trauma?

The answers to these questions should inform all aspects of the patient's treatment. Therapists work to assure the victims that they are in no way responsible for being attacked, assaulted, and abused. This not only creates a safe environment where the patient can begin to address their experience but also makes it more likely that other victims will feel safe coming forward. Doctors also focus on trauma as an underlying issue in other conditions.

It is only in recent human history that we have healed our sick through myopic means. It is time for a pivot back to a "whole person" treatment approach. In integrated care, the staff work collectively to address all aspects of patients' health. Coming from a variety of behavioral, medical, and administrative specialties, their pooled expertise, and efforts are central to the provision of integrated care. Their responsibilities can be broken down into five categories.

The role of the care team in integrated care is, first and foremost, to diagnose and treat illness. But unlike in traditional healthcare, in integrated care, this diagnosis and treatment occurs as early as possible and is highly individualized to the patient's psyche and life experience. The other four responsibility categories are care management, information collection, care team communication, and health promotion.

There are a variety of methods for clinically aligning behavioral health and primary care. These methods include cross-training for problem identification, formally diagnosing conditions, and treating the spectrum of disease states. Additional methods for clinical alignment include having continuous consultative services available, having strategies for increasing patient's health literacy which enhances engagement and activation by informed providers who are anticipating behavioral health care needs that are individualized, and delivering a team-based care system. Best practices include co-locating services when possible and utilizing formal assessment screenings in even trans-organizational settings.

I am not the first person to declare the importance of this approach. Experts in both behavioral and whole-health care have been calling for a multidisciplinary approach for years. I am not even the first person to implement it. And I am just one in a chorus of voices saying now is the time to scale it up.

We all have, at one time or another, failed to recognize a major historical change while it was happening. In most of these moments of significance, it is nearly impossible to seize the moment for the betterment of our lives.

I am questioning myself here—but sometimes I ask myself why I did not buy Microsoft stock at $21 when it first came out in 1986. I could code. I was relatively computer-savvy for the 80s. Why I did not see the significance of this little startup in Redmond, Washington?

I am not saying I should have fully grasped Bill Gates' vision for the personal computer. Maybe I never could have suspected that these machines would surround us in various forms today. But maybe I could have reasonably appreciated the potential of the business model.

After buying the code for what would eventually be MS-DOS for probably $10,000, Gates had begun licensing it to IBM and others. He would pursue this market until almost 90% of the world's PCs relied on his software. Then, of course, there are the desktop applications (I am typing this manuscript in Word right now), the web browser, enterprise software, video game consoles, etc. The company is still going strong today.

I, of course, anticipated none of this. To be fair, much of it was beyond even Bill Gates' vision. But this, in a way, is the call to action I am making to healthcare business leaders in this book.

Not to buy stock and get rich. Not literally, at least. But to capitalize on the potential for an investment that all of us in the healthcare industry should reasonably have the ability to anticipate.

I am speaking to healthcare providers and healthcare business leaders. There is a better model of care out there. Investing in this model will accrue tremendous benefits for both you and your patients. And it is available to you now. The IPO is today.

The most effective model of healthcare is the one that seamlessly integrates the treatment of physical and behavioral health disorders. And if you will take steps to implement truly integrated care today, it will transform your organization into a center of excellence. It will make you a healthcare thought leader. And in three decades, you will have generated tremendous wealth—in terms of impact on the lives of your patients and their families.

Addiction is a great illustration of the impact that integrated care can have on patients, on your career, and on your business. That is because addiction is something that is easily understood as a problem with medical, psychological, and myriad other roots.

Substance use disorders reduce functioning to a simplistic state. Addiction traps people in a pattern of fundamentally under-utilizing their humanity. They lack complexity in their focus. In the worst—but unfortunately not rare—case, they are spending all their time procuring the drug, being high, or recovering from its effects. Despite this simplistic existence, addiction is an exceedingly complicated disease. It requires a diverse and coordinated range of psychosocial therapies and medical interventions to treat.

It is impossible to discuss the need for coordinated addiction treatment without establishing the fact that addiction is an "integrated disease." It affects every aspect and cell of one's physical, mental, and spiritual life. Effectively treating addiction often means deconstructing a patient's psyche, uncovering and understanding unaddressed or repressed trauma, and building new systems of belief—all while treating the physical/genetic forces of alcohol and other substances.

Addiction and existential crisis often go hand in hand, and the disease is as much a philosophical illness as a mental and physical one. Perhaps no other field of medicine attempts to treat a more complex set of symptoms and underlying causes, and no other area of medicine requires as holistic and integrated an approach to produce successful outcomes than that of treating addiction.

Consider this latest article on the assessment of addictive disorders from a neuroscience-based framework when reflecting on the complexity of interventions required to treat such a profound disease state. To address the reality of heterogeneity of etiology, the authors identify genetic variables, environmental variables, agent use history, and impact on functionality as primary domains to consider while accounting for one's cognitive control, negative emotionality, and incentive salience. Despite this comprehensive model, they posited "given the multifactorial nature of addictive disorders, changing nature of exposure and response of human populations to addictive agents, the anticipated development of new methods for treatment and prevention, and development of new, transformative technologies, we do not anticipate that any one functional domain or imaging or genetic predictor will resolve the heterogeneity of addictive disorders or be sufficient to characterize an individual patient" (Kwako, 2015).

Clearly, addiction treatment calls for a multidisciplinary, collaborative care model that only integrated care can provide. Integrated care is your 1986 Microsoft stock. Implementing this model of care will pay dividends—both in your career as a provider and in the lives of the people you treat.

But why is the IPO today? This care model has been around for a while. What is the rush?

The need for integrated care is magnified right now by the addiction crisis in America. The current crisis is being driven by opioid use and a more recent surge in stimulants, which has increased dramatically in recent years.

The latest contributing supply and demand vectors have spiked in the past eight years with nationwide overdose deaths for cocaine and psychostimulants reaching almost 25,000 in 2017, with the rate of deaths from cocaine tripling and deaths from psychostimulants increasing fivefold. This epidemic includes both prescribed and illicit substance use disorders. Despite the high numbers of those dealing with this epidemic, they are still far outweighed by the number of people suffering from alcoholism, with roughly four times (95,000) as many alcohol-related deaths annually between 2011 and 2015 as these drug-related deaths each year. And substance use rates have increased during the COVID-19 pandemic.

The seriousness of this long-standing problem demands an integrated approach. And the effort and expense of implementing this approach is justified—even just for the benefit of bringing more attention to the public. Under integrated care, more healthcare professionals are going to be looking for the clues that a patient is abusing substances. It heightens attention to the problem.

So yes, addiction is a perfect demonstration of the impact of—and the urgency for—integrated care. In truth, however, addiction is not unique in this regard. All illnesses have a complex area of factors at play. At the beginning of the pandemic, we sought the pie-in-the-sky solution. The cure.

A year in, however, it was clear that mortality associated with COVID-19 will continue to be determined by a mixture of vaccines, various medications and other treatments, masks, social distancing, comorbidities, and lifestyle—such as diet, exercise, and tobacco use. And then you have also got to think about risk factors that are beyond our control, such as genetics and age.

If only there was some kind of investment we could make in our healthcare system! Something that would pay off in impact on as many determinants of health as possible. Again, Bill Gates comes to mind.

"If anything kills over 10 million people over the next few decades, it is likely to be a highly infectious virus rather than a war," Gates told his audience at a TED Talk five years before the pandemic.

In Gates' decades-long journey from a young billionaire tech entrepreneur to a major voice of global health, I wonder if he ever thought he would be accused of spreading a virus so that he could sell people a vaccine that would allow him to surveil their every move. I suspect that, too, was beyond his vision of the future.

2020 was a disaster in many ways, and one of them was the messaging around the science and public health of COVID-19. I can understand how these conspiracies spread. There was a captive audience. Everyone was very anxious. We desperately sought a feeling of control in our lives, and the pandemic confronted us every day with the fact that none of us were in control.

So, some of us attempted to assume a false mastery over information. They were seeking information that simply did not exist yet. On top of that, our political and public health leaders did a poor job of disseminating information, and so a lot of good information and expertise was discredited in the eyes of the public.

Therefore, the public sought information from many different media—television, websites, Facebook, YouTube, and TikTok. And the usual interpersonal exchanges disappeared because of social isolation. So, at the same time that we were inundated with information, it became more of a challenge for people to discern the veracity of each piece of information. That very process of vetting was overwhelming.

Simplicity and survival led straight into distortion. And the results were heartbreaking to watch.

The anxiety, powerlessness, and confusion of the COVID-19 pandemic are much like the way patients with substance use disorder feel all the time, especially when bouncing around the dysfunctional avenues of our healthcare system. Unable to get an appointment. Unable to get coverage. Unable to get transportation. Unable to get information.

But it does not have to be this way. Integrated care greatly improves the delivery of healthcare. That is not just because it addresses multiple dimensions of disease, but also because it enables early intervention. Integrated care empowers providers to diagnose earlier in the progress of a disorder when treatment is generally more effective. In addition, integrated care results in a better patient experience and patient engagement, which are powerful fuels for the business success of health systems and centers. It empowers patients in a system that makes them feel a lack of control. It reduces churn and burnout among healthcare employees.

And finally, integrated care reduces disparities that exist across racial and ethnic groups—but it is not enough. Healthcare leaders implementing this model must also consciously consider racial and ethnic bias and discrimination. The role of recurrent, systemic, and pervasive traumas experienced by individuals, communities, and societies requires a sensitive response that avoids further victimization and marginalization. So yes, the hard work of addressing bias and racism must be done as well, but integrated care is the best model of care for delivering equitable care.

The barriers are high. Implementing integrated care in your system or practice will not happen overnight. But all of these barriers can be lowered. I have done it, and you can too.

This book will focus on the barriers that primary care and behavioral health professionals can influence. And just like patients, doctors and even healthcare executives can feel powerless in the bureaucracy of healthcare. But you will be surprised what influence you have! Providers and healthcare business leaders do have some power to overcome incompatible EHR systems, insurance coverage limits, and other seemingly intractable problems.

This book will give you tools to fight back against resistance from management, providers, referral sources and support staff, and insurance companies—but most importantly, to secure buy-in from business leadership and primary care providers. I will also talk about how to tackle some myths that stand in your way with important stakeholders. One of the most widely held fallacies is that integrated care will increase PCPs' workload and decrease the time available to spend with patients. Not true!

Another stubborn myth is that having good technology is enough to enable collaboration. Indeed, data-informed decision-making, great EHRs and communication tools, and other technology improvements are critical ingredients for integrated care. This measurement-based care model includes comprehensive assessments that generate tons of data that needs to be shared. It includes telehealth. It ideally includes components of artificial intelligence, matching interventions with specific disorders. All of this is incredibly helpful. But technology alone is not going to get you here.

And a final myth I will dig into is the idea that integrated care is all or nothing. This model can be implemented in a variety of settings—from large systems to independent practices. Ideally, you would have the budget to hire more staff and build out your facility, but I will also talk about adopting integrated care across different organizations and locations.

Integrated care involves the provision of medical care in a behavioral health setting and the provision of behavioral health in a medical setting. The intent is to provide early diagnosis and treatment of mental health problems, to increase access to medical care for those with mental illnesses, and to improve the overall health of the population served. Although the goal is the full merging of the two services in a seamless organization, the reality is that implementation happens along a spectrum. It ranges from little coordination all the way to complete integration.

This orchestrated effort results in ideal services being delivered by the integrated team. And it is not just the individual patient that is receiving care, but their family and other systems to which they belong. Integrated care has a ripple effect, spreading outward from the patient.

This effect mirrors the groupings to which humans belong throughout their life cycle. When you are born, you have a small group of guardians taking care of you. As you start to become more independent, that group expands to include kindergarten teachers and other caregivers. As you grow, you recognize the differences in the people who belong to your ever-widening circles, and you develop attachments to a broader suite of them—not only other caregivers but also peers. When done well, the impact of integrated care mirrors the complexity of systems that you encounter as you grow developmentally.

Integrated care takes into account the incredibly valuable contributions made by each member of the team, models healthy communication and affects regulation, and is sensitive to the patient's unique needs and desires. This care is fundamentally respectful to the patient because it takes their whole experience and every determinant of health into consideration, instead of just reducing them to a few elements focused on an illness state. To actually explore and question these comprehensive variables offers an individual a multisystemic framework for their condition. Integrated care is accountable. Integrated care providers have a higher quality of professionalism.

Integrated care partners with individuals in a collaborative process that enhances healing. When individuals feel like they are part of the solution, regardless of the condition or disease, they believe their patterns of health and healing are understandable and achievable. Life's stressors do not seem so insurmountable, which translates into a fulfillment of the healthcare vision. When motivation is high and treatment readiness is improved, social support improves. When rapport is maximized, patients who had not paid attention to their health become more compliant with their providers. Social desirability replaces personal irresponsibility (Institute of Behavioral Research, 2007).

Integrated care is an investment in your future and in the future of all the patients who will walk through your doors.

Today is the IPO for your winning stock. And the return will be greater than you think.

Reference

Institute of Behavioral Research. (2007). TCU social functioning (TCU SOCForm). Forth Worth. Retrieved from TCU College of Science & Engineering: https://ibr.tcu.edu/forms/client-evaluation-of-self-and-treatment-cest/

2 History of Integrated Care and Addiction

It is not easy to notice the historical significance of the moment in which you are living. It is much harder to seize that moment for a better future. Luckily, sometimes you land on a team that helps seize it for you.

In the late 1980s, fresh out of an undergraduate psychology program and having missed the opportunity to get rich off Microsoft stock, I took a job in what I assumed would be a lower-growth market.

I went to work at a large private behavioral health treatment facility. Four psychiatrists who were doing trailblazing work in mental healthcare founded the hospital. I did not realize at the time how important their approach was or the effect it would have in shaping my understanding of mental healthcare or indeed its effect on the field as a whole. I had no way of knowing I was getting in on the ground floor of a revolution in the treatment of mental illnesses and addiction.

At the time, most psychiatric care was rather one-dimensional. Patients were admitted and treated for primary problems. Those with depression received depression treatment. People with sexual dysfunctions had their dysfunction addressed. Those who were admitted for emotional trauma received counseling for that. The idea that you should be addressing co-occurring disorders, physical conditions, and mental health issues with addictive disorders was not widespread.

But this treatment center was employing a new socialized approach rooted in evidence-based care. It was an early adopter of what we would now call integrated care.

Before describing what should be the next step in addiction treatment, it is imperative to review the stages the industry has endured throughout history, as this current model has been built on the shoulders of many.

History of Addiction Treatment

Addiction treatment has moved from seeing substance abuse as a moral problem to recognizing it as a disease with a complicated etiology compounded by co-occurring disorders. However, the path from one to the other has not been a straight line. Numerous approaches to dealing with

DOI: 10.4324/9781003128571-2

substance use disorders have been tried. Some came and went quickly, yet others would see a resurgence from time to time. Multiple streams of thought have merged and diverged en route to our current place in addiction treatment.

The need to deal with those who overindulge in intoxicating substances is at least as old as written history. Beer and wine were staples of the diets in both Egypt and Mesopotamia. Along with warnings of the dangers of drunkenness were concerns about the ready availability of alcohol. The Bible, of course, contains exhortations against drinking too much. And despite their generally tolerant attitudes toward excessive drinking in Greece and Rome, they still recognized that it could be a detriment to those who engaged in it, including those that have given us perhaps some of the greatest works known to our species during the Renaissance. All societies throughout history have regarded drunkenness as a problem on one level or another regardless of the high praise of intellectuals and artists.

In the United States, the problem predates the founding of the nation. But it was in the first half-century after the Revolutionary War that the problem of substance abuse became acute. Before and during the war, beer, cider, and wine were the primary drinks of choice. Hard liquor was present—particularly New England rum—but was nowhere near as common.

After America won its independence, the production and consumption of distilled spirits rose at an unprecedented rate. The opening of land west of the Appalachians brought fresh farmland, and farmers frequently used their excess grain (e.g., corn, barley, and rye) to produce whiskey. From 1790 to 1830, the consumption of hard liquor rose precipitously as per-capita alcohol consumption rose from 2.5 gallons in 1792 to 4.5 gallons in 1810 and finally to 7.1 gallons in 1830 (White, 2014). This brought with it a concomitant rise in dipsomania (a term used at the time for alcoholism). People noticed the increase and decided to do something about it.

As a generalization, three groups of approaches that can be attributed to the problem of addiction are temperance movements, mutual aid groups, and professional treatment. These have usually existed side by side, each in turn waxing and waning in popularity. Although temperance movements fell on hard times following the disaster of Prohibition, all three inform modern treatment and warrant mentioning.

Temperance Movements

The first temperance movements in the US began in the late eighteenth and early nineteenth centuries. They were attempts to curtail the amount of drunkenness through the use of "persuasion." Although some of these movements were religious in nature, some simply focused on the damages to individuals and society caused by alcohol. While some began by espousing moderation, by 1830, most moved to a call for complete abstinence. These movements approached dipsomaniacs, hoping to convince them to stop drinking. Seldom did the movement advocate laws banning alcohol.

As the nineteenth century progressed, hopes of curbing the drinking of alcohol through the use of persuasion faded, and reformers began to seek more coercive means. Some early efforts were successful in Maine, which passed a law in 1851 prohibiting the sale of all alcohol except for alcohol used for "medicinal, mechanical or manufacturing purposes." The law was repealed in 1856. About a dozen other states tried to pass similar laws, but these were either vetoed, overturned by the courts, or found to be unenforceable (Okrent, 2010).

It was not until the 1870s, however, that the temperance movement started to see true success in its attempts to legislate alcohol. At the forefront were two movements: The Women's Christian Temperance Union (WCTU) and the Anti-Saloon League. These associations attempted to fight alcohol on both the state and national level, and their success led to the passage of the 18th Amendment and the start of Prohibition.

Their mission was so closely tied to Prohibition, however, that they both lost considerable influence with the failure of Prohibition and its repeal. In certain cities, the failure was particularly dramatic. My hometown of New Orleans was called "the liquor capital of America" during Prohibition (Magill, 2018). With the production of homebrews and foreign liquor being smuggled into the city being so prolific, one observer said, "We all seemed to feel that prohibition was a personal affront and that we had a moral duty to undermine it." The distribution and delivery seemed to tap into bar and restaurants' creativity. "A wink for a drink if you were known" was the rule, curbside demitasses with mixers on the side were available, and the police showed little motivation and only half-hearted attempts to make arrests.

On August 11, 1925, the "clean-up of New Orleans" took place when 200 out-of-town agents staged a series of sensational raids, among the most important in the history of Prohibition. The agents uncovered 10,000 cases of liquor, and some said they had never seen so much alcohol, even before Prohibition. There was still so much hidden liquor in New Orleans that one bootlegger scoffed at the haul, telling the local newspaper, *Times-Picayune*, that the agents "didn't get such an awful amount. I don't believe the price of liquor in New Orleans will go up much" (Magill, 2018).

The popular view of the temperance movement is that they were moralists wanting to stop people from having fun. In reality, many members were involved because they had witnessed first-hand the damage caused by alcoholism—which, to this day, continues to be the driving force behind policies, laws, and treatment strategies. Many women participated in the WCTU because they had been harmed by the drinking of their husbands. They were tired of having their husbands spend all their money at a bar on payday. They and their children had experienced abuse at the hands of angry husbands who came home drunk. And they watched as alcoholism slowly destroyed the ability of their husbands to earn a living. In many ways, the WCTU was just as much about women's empowerment as the Suffrage Movement that began at the same time.

In fact, many women were members of both movements. These women were not just social reformers; they were also trying to deal with the impact of alcohol on their families. They were the first interventionists of our times.

Mutual Aid Societies and an Early Asylum

Another approach to the problem of addiction came from individuals who gave up drinking and banded together to support each other in sobriety. One of the earliest and best-known mutual aid societies was the Washingtonians. The Washingtonians were formed by a group of six men in Baltimore in 1840. Having attended a temperance lecture, the six of them decided to band together in a pledge of abstinence.

The idea was not just that they would each abstain from drinking, but also that they would help each other stick to that promise. Each of them also vowed to seek out other inebriates and encourage them to join the movement. It grew rapidly and spread to other cities. Members attended large, revival-style meetings where they heard the stories of others affected by alcohol and how they had changed. Many would come forward weeping, eager to sign the pledge.

The movement was built on the twin ideas that alcoholics could change themselves and that they did it best with the help of other alcoholics, ideas that would form part of most mutual aid societies, including Alcoholics Anonymous (AA). Within a few years, membership had grown as high as 600,000 men. An auxiliary group, the Martha Washingtonians, was founded for women.

Unfortunately, the Washingtonians disappeared as quickly as they appeared. By 1847, the only Washingtonian society still in operation was in Boston. Several factors led to their decline. Partly to blame was the initial intensity of the movement, which could not be sustained. The founders frequently traveled a circuit of cities delivering their message, and the travel took its toll. It may also have suffered from the burnout that frequently plagues movements built primarily on enthusiasm. Some religious organizations also objected to the Washingtonians, noting that their fervor did not leave much room for God.

Although the Washingtonians came and went quickly, the idea of mutual support remained, most notably in the inebriate asylums and homes that began to be founded in the 1850s. One aspect of these asylums—intentionally or unintentionally—was the mutual support the patients provided to one another. In time, it extended beyond the patients to the staff, as many of them were men who had come through treatment themselves. Over time, the line between patient and staff became blurred, as patients were encouraged to engage in work for the asylum while they recovered.

This foreshadows the type of mutual support that is found in many modern addiction treatment centers, where people who have finished the program sometimes return to be mentors and recovery coaches, as well as offer peer support to others. Obviously, professionals in the addiction field with live experiences offer rich compassion, commitment, and caring to those in need.

Nowhere is the mutual support model more clearly seen than in the Keeley Institute, which was founded in 1879. It is often known for its controversial Keeley Gold Cure which was rejected by most medical professionals at the time as injectables could not be responsible for treatment outcomes such as alcoholism.

The Keeley Institute is also known for being one of the first franchised substance use treatment centers. And its high success rate at its main facility in Dwight, Illinois, cannot be denied. Some attribute this success to the camaraderie that developed between the men as they waited in line four times a day to receive their shots of the "cure." It was also common for current patients to go to the train station each day to welcome new arrivals. This shared experience in recovery developed strong bonds, and the men often continued to support each other after leaving the institute.

The best-known mutual assistance groups are AA and its spin-offs (for example, Narcotics Anonymous) that help those addicted to other substances.

The history of AA is well documented. Founded in 1935 by William Griffith Wilson and Dr. Robert Smith (a.k.a. Bill and Dr. Bob), the group works to help others through meetings where people share their stories and support one another. To facilitate recovery, AA members work the 12 Steps, and members in long-term recovery serve as sponsors to those in the early stages. Although it does not advocate any particular religion or denomination, AA does include a focus on a "higher power," an aspect absent from the Washingtonians' approach (Wilson, 1957).

Professional Treatment

Professional approaches to addiction treatment include both medical and psychological approaches, that is, those who prescribe medications for treatment and those who use therapy and analysis. These, however, are modern divisions, and early approaches to addiction by professionals did not distinguish between the two. What differentiated professionals from the temperance movement and mutual aid societies was an attempt to use scientific principles to understand, diagnose, and treat substance use disorders.

A pioneer in this field was Benjamin Rush, who practiced both medicine and psychology. In addition to being a Founding Father of the United States, he is also considered the father of American psychiatry and the father of addiction treatment. He was so influential in this field, in fact, that his image is used as the center of the seal of the American Psychiatric Association. In addition to cataloging mental illnesses, Rush was one of the first to espouse the idea that addiction is a disease instead of a moral failing. His study "An Inquiry into the Effects of Ardent Spirits upon the Human Body and Mind" was one of the first to attempt to understand alcoholism as a physical and mental condition.

Despite Rush's influence, the treatment of addiction remained in its infancy until the development of inebriate asylums in the second half of the nineteenth century. These asylums, modeled on the insane asylums of the time, were the first to attempt to treat alcoholism as a mental disorder. Several were founded throughout the country, with those in New York, Boston, Philadelphia, and Chicago being the best known while Southern cities appeared to be slower to adopt. One of their guiding principles was that men needed to be removed from their normal living and working situation to focus on recovery—an idea still embraced by inpatient/residential facilities today.

Treatment in the inebriate asylums was primarily psychiatric, although medical doctors were employed to help people during the initial stage of detoxification. Instead of stopping substance use suddenly, the patients were often either weaned off alcohol slowly or given some other substance—such as opium—to help them through the withdrawal symptoms. Most asylums subscribed to the idea that drunkenness was caused by neurological problems in the brain, an idea common during this period. Treatment consisted of talk therapy, exercise, fresh air, therapeutic communities, and water treatments to rejuvenate one's body.

Many patients were also encouraged to participate in the operation of the asylum by doing chores. In addition, the nonjudgmental fellowship of others in the same situation and encouragement by former patients now employed by the asylum created the mutual support network discussed earlier.

Inebriate asylums were the first major attempt to provide public assistance to alcoholics, as most asylums were state-run. Although some patients were committed to the asylums against their will, others were there voluntarily. A separate, private system existed alongside the asylums. Generally known as "inebriate homes," these organizations were run by individual organizations and supported by donations. They were often closely connected to temperance movements. Although these two types of institutions represent a step forward in addiction treatment, both ceased to exist with the passage of Prohibition. Once it became illegal to drink, the funding completely dried up for the medical treatment of alcoholism. Public perception shifted, and dipsomania was viewed as a crime rather than a disease.

After the repeal of Prohibition, treatment of alcoholism—and increasingly the treatment of other substances addictions such as heroin and cocaine—entered a period of intellectual growth. Numerous models were proposed from both the medical and psychological fields. These models were intended both to explain addiction and to provide insight into the proper methods of treatment. Hester (1990) discuss the models that were used in the second half of the twentieth century:

- Disease model: Viewed alcoholism as a progressive, incurable disease characterized by a lack of control over drinking. Because addiction was a disease and not a moral failure, this model called for intervention instead of incarceration
- Educational models: Addiction is caused by a lack of understanding of the harmful effects of substance use. Therefore, education is the key to preventing and healing addiction
- Characterological models: These models saw the roots of addiction in personality disorders, often couched in Freudian terms of fixation in specific stages of development that prevent complex maturity. These models advocated psychoanalysis
- Conditioning models: Addiction is a learned behavior. The solution is the reconditioning of the habits by behavioral therapists
- Biological models: These saw people as being genetically predisposed to alcoholism. They called for caution in people from families with a history of alcoholism. Treatment was usually medical in nature
- Systems models: Alcoholism is caused by the systems in which an individual operates. A dysfunctional family system, for example, could enable addiction. The family system must be healed for the addict to achieve recovery. Family and systems therapists were the primary modes of treatment
- Sociocultural models: These models posit that societal factors are the biggest contributors to addiction. Education of the public and legislation regulating substances is the best way to address substance use disorders
- Public health model: Addiction should be treated as any other public health concern by focusing on the agent, host, and environment. This model seeks to pull together several of the other models, recognizing that substance use disorders are complex conditions that have multiple contributing factors

At first, some of these models were used individually, particularly by those who developed them. One single approach was seen as being the key to unlocking the problem of addiction. As we approached the end of the twentieth century, some of these models began to be used in tandem. Such combined treatments set the stage for contemporary addiction treatment (Kelly, 2018).

Today, the DSM-5 encompasses 10 separate classes of drugs: Alcohol; caffeine; tobacco, cannabis; hallucinogens; inhalants; opioids; sedatives; stimulants; and other (or unknown) substances. Two distinct conditions include substance use disorders and substance intoxication and withdrawal with a need to consider a differential diagnosis for all relevant diagnoses. Overall, a pathological pattern of behaviors related to the use of substances is grouped into impaired control, social impairment, risky use, and pharmacological criteria. So, individuals may take larger amounts or over a longer period than was originally intended while expressing a desire to cut down or regulate substance use. They report multiple unsuccessful efforts to decrease or discontinue their use while spending a significant amount of time procuring, using, or recovering from its effects. Cravings are present with an intense desire or urge for the substance when in an environment where the substance was previously used. Social impairment is present with a failure to fulfill major role obligations at work, school, or interpersonal relationships. Also, these social, occupational, or recreational activities are given up or reduced because of use including reduced family engagement. Risky use includes physically dangerous situations and having persistent or recurring physical or psychological problems. Finally, tolerance and withdrawal are characteristic symptoms of the pharmacological criteria but are excluded when medical treatment is occurring.

The severity specifiers range from mild to severe depending on the number of symptoms present when diagnosing a substance use disorder. In addition, "in early remission," "in sustained remission," "on maintenance therapy," and "in a controlled environment" round out the specifiers (American Psychiatric Association, 2013).

The Fall and Rise of Integrated Care

During the twentieth century, as addiction treatment was making leaps and bounds toward a more effective model, integration of care was sliding backward.

The concept of integrated care is based on the principle that the best healthcare requires treating the person as a whole. In the past, this was the norm. Aside from the occasional need for a hospital stay for serious illnesses or injuries, someone could receive all their care from one local doctor's office, which is similar to veterinary medicine today. Even if the practice employed several physicians, the centralization ensured that information was shared with everyone involved in the care process. For better and worse, those days have disappeared.

Several factors led medicine to move away from this model during the twentieth century. One of the primary influences was the increasing amount of knowledge needed to treat patients. As advancements were made in our understanding of the human body, it became impossible for one person or even a single practice to know enough to provide all forms of care. Medical fields became increasingly specialized as research produced more and more granular knowledge. Because the body of literature produced grew exponentially, general practitioners who served as PCPs could not be expected to stay current at more than a cursory level.

Just as the industrial revolution led to the separation of different portions of the manufacturing process, so the increased specialization of knowledge led healthcare to be divided into multiple practices. Under the simple heading of "doctor," we came to have cardiologists, dermatologists, neurologists, oncologists, and podiatrists. Specialties were developed for various ages (e.g., pediatrics, geriatrics) and genders (e.g., gynecology, urology). And, of course, medical and surgical specialists were separate from mental health providers.

This approach has its benefits. Doctors who focus on one area of study can go much deeper in their understanding and stay current in that field. Specialists' offices can have the equipment they need without having to worry about devices for other fields. Patients receive better treatment because they are being seen by someone who deals with their particular problem regularly instead of a general practitioner who has seen their condition only once or twice in their practice.

The drawback to this division is the siloization of treatment. Under this system, different parts of the person are treated, while the person as a whole is often ignored.

Like a contractor who only does plumbing, specialists deal with only one type of problem. Patients with multiple conditions have to make appointments to see several doctors at several facilities, usually on several different days. Although the treatment for those particular issues is better, it was likely that conditions not covered by each specialist are set aside for someone else to handle—if they are even diagnosed at all.

The converse of this is also possible. Instead of a condition being undiagnosed or ignored, multiple specialists can be treating the same disease, each being unaware of the other's care. Among other problems, this could lead to multiple medications being prescribed for the same condition, a phenomenon known as polypharmacy. This raises the possibility of drug interactions that have undesirable or even deadly effects. And different specialists sometimes administer treatments that work against one another, thereby reducing or nullifying their efficacy.

River Oaks opened for inpatient care in New Orleans in 1970. The expansion of programs, staff, and physical plant occurred over the 13 years for the hospital, which was once an 80-bed unit at DePaul in New Orleans. Founded by a group of local psychiatrists including Drs. John A. Stocks, William R. Sorum, Robert W. Davis, Alfred Olinde,

John Paul Pratt, Sam Benbow, Jacob Weisler, and Judge Morey L. Sear, the hospital maintained a high quality of treatment programs with its specialty of long-term intensive psychotherapy for adolescents and young adults, with limited use of medication. Nestled in a crook of the "Big Muddy," River Oaks Hospital opened a new facility in 1983 which offered an integrated care model.

In the 1970s, Robert Davis, MD, had taken a personal journey and studied abroad to find out about the impact of social agents related to milieu therapy, which was people living in the same context, creating a community, displaying different roles through assignment or by natural progression, and the power of exchange related to this social atom. In that context, healthcare providers could take care of the whole person with multiple modalities and therapeutic interventions by a whole team of professionals with numerous specialties (i.e., psychiatrist, general practitioners, nurses, psychologists, social workers, dance and movement therapist, art therapist, psychodrama professionals, music therapist, occupational therapist, and physical therapist). An array of services was offered to the patient and their families which enhanced functioning of life skills with minimal use of medication aids.

With a new facility, his own unit, and partners with numerous specialties including addiction treatment, he was poised to continue delivering exceptional care of the whole person.

These professionals who started the Trauma Program at River Oaks were trained in several fields, including trauma, addiction, sexuality, eating disorders, personality, and mood disorders. Although having several specialties in one practice was common in behavioral health, the closeness with which they collaborated was not. Patients admitted with a particular diagnosis would also be screened for other conditions. Psychological testing was performed on every patient admitted and any co-occurring disorders would then be treated alongside the initial problem. They also included a focus on the patients' physical health by consulting with staff physicians specializing in Internal or Family medicine. Most were also trained in addiction and/or psychiatry as well. They dealt with extremely complicated cases with an integrated team of professionals, a novel approach at the time. The treatment center encouraged experimentation with movement, music, and art therapies, innovation, research, and evidence-based therapies.

The work helped establish many of the concepts that now enjoy widespread use, including stigma reduction, addressing trauma with every patient, believing each life experience, and a focus on physical health and wellness. The Trauma Program at River Oaks was one of the centers that laid the foundation for the field of sexual abuse treatment. However, a great deal of work still must be done to remove the stigma of sexual assault.

I arrived at River Oaks in 1989. I found a patient population consisting primarily of people with an identified history of sexual trauma and sexual compulsive disorders. Some of the work and research I was doing was under the direct tutelage of William Masters, MD—one-half of the well-known research team Masters and Johnson. Dr. Masters is world-renowned for his work in sexual functioning and sex therapy during the 1950s through the 1990s. Together he and Virginia Johnson founded the field of sex therapy.

Working with Dr. Masters and his scholarly protégés provided me with an understanding of the complexity of human sexuality. Each individual's expression of sexuality—whether healthy, indifferent, or aberrant—are influenced by a multitude of factors. Genetics, childhood experiences, cultural and social influences, and past relationships all interact to form how we think of ourselves and express our sexual scripts. They set the bounds on the subgroup of people to whom we are attracted, the types of fantasies we have, the things that excite us, and the behaviors in which we engage.

Dr. Masters understood that treating people with sexual dysfunctions required addressing multiple facets of the problem. Because the condition is an integration of many factors, treatment must be integrated as well. In understanding the underlying causes of sexual dysfunction, it is not possible to simply identify one primary factor and ignore other issues. With so many factors involved (e.g., cultural influences, natural development, past trauma, physical issues, self-image, relationships, and a host of other elements), he and my other mentors encouraged innovation and experimentation with integrated approaches that touched on all aspects of the patient's well-being.

This approach is not just beneficial for sexual disorders—it is appropriate for all forms of mental health disorders. This is the case because of the complexity of the mind. Just as multiple factors influence our expression of sexuality, all aspects of behavior and personality involve the confluence of culture, genetics, experiences, and physical health, among other components. This means that an approach to addiction treatment that focuses on only one aspect—whether it be physical dependence, chronic pain, past trauma, or genetic predisposition—will fail to adequately address the complexity of the disease. Only by treating the entire person and dealing with all facets of the disease of addiction can we give patients the level of care they deserve.

The Trauma Program at River Oaks' success illustrated the effectiveness of the approach heralded by Dr. Davis, Dr. Schwartz, Dr. Masters, Dan Glaser, Lori Galperin, and others. We had a roughly six-month waiting list to help people from all over the country deal with deep, traumatic wounds. And that success allowed our team to scale up the model to the broader UHS system, which had acquired the hospital in 1983.

In the last 20 years, addiction treatment has improved the level of care provided, as evident by the development and implementation of such criteria as that offered by the American Society of Addiction Medicine (ASAM). Previously, licensing was enough to allow someone to be hired by a treatment center. As the industry has matured, however, a greater focus on education and training has been seen. Along with the growing skill set of treatment providers has come an increased recognition of the complexity of addiction. They have led to the development of multidisciplinary approaches to the treatment of substance use disorders. And although modern analysis and psychiatry had been previously resisted, they have become accepted parts of addiction treatment.

On a parallel path, in recent decades, medicine has begun to move away from its siloization and toward a model of integrated care (O'Donahue, Cummings, Cucciare, Runyan, & Cummings, 2006). Primary care providers are increasingly seen as the ones who are in charge of overseeing the care process, to ensure that one person is responsible for the overall direction of treatment. They maintain the patient-centered care team, which allows individuals to feel grounded during their care.

The technological capacity has facilitated this integration with electronic health record (EHR) systems making the sharing and documenting of patient information much easier. While medicine has evolved to include specializations in data science, health systems management, and population health, and while there has been some movement in the direction of care coordination, the field still has progress to make. This is especially true in regard to integration with behavioral health.

The passage of legislation has not, however, resulted in high service delivery of behavioral healthcare within the primary care systems.

The Current Addiction Crises

Alcohol, of course, is not the only addiction crisis that our country has struggled to reign in. Previous stimulant crises centered on crack cocaine in the 1980s and crystal meth in the 1990s and 2000s.

Cadet and Gold (2017) report a serious public health problem with a recreational use estimated at 35.7 million people around the world with various routes of admission. This misuse can cause psychiatric diseases that resemble naturally occurring illnesses but are more difficult to treat. Long-term exposure has been shown to cause severe neurotoxic and neuropathological effects. Psychosis can be induced in 13–50% of the individuals using methamphetamine with the difference related to the purity of the substance used. These conditions may have a lasting effect and could also result in cognitive abnormalities.

The roots of today's opioid crisis can be traced to an increased willingness on the part of doctors to prescribe opioids as pain relievers. The rise has been rapid and dramatic.

Opioids used as analgesics include morphine (MS Contin), oxycodone

(OxyContin), and hydrocodone (Vicodin). Before the 1990s, such substances were used almost exclusively to deal with cancer-related pain. But starting shortly before the turn of the twenty-first century, doctors began to prescribe opioids more frequently for acute pain not related to cancer. In addition to using opioids to address acute pain, the number of medical practitioners using them to treat chronic pain has also risen.

Opioid prescriptions jumped from 76 million prescriptions in 1991 to 217 million in 2012 (National Institute of Drug Abuse, 2014) and a peak rate of 81.3 prescriptions per 100 persons in 2012 (Centers for Disease Control and Prevention, 2018). From 2000 to 2010, opioid analgesic prescriptions increased by 104%, with the number of Americans taking prescription opioids rising from 7.4% in 2000 to 11.8% in 2010 (Sites, 2014). In 2015, doctors prescribed three times the amount of opioids that they did in 1999 (Centers for Disease Control and Prevention, 2020c). Despite the dramatic reduction of opioid prescriptions between 2012 and 2017, 17.4% of the U.S. population reported having one or more opioid prescriptions within the past year and the average person received 3.4 prescriptions.

Because of the inherent risk of addiction when dealing with opioids, the increase in prescriptions was bound to inflate the number of people with substance use disorders (Edlund, 2014). A study by the Centers for Disease Control and Prevention indicated that risk of addiction began with as little as one day of use and "that racial and ethnic minority groups, women, the elderly, persons with cognitive impairment, and those with cancer and at the end of life, can be at risk for inadequate pain treatment" (Centers for Disease Control and Prevention, 2020a). Significant jumps in the likelihood of addiction came at three, five, and thirty days. Even when used as medically indicated, opioids always carry with them a chance of patients developing a substance use disorder.

Some patients who take prescribed opioid medications in the long term can be unaware that they have developed an addiction. This is particularly the case for people who are taking opioids for chronic pain. Such patients can develop a syndrome known as hyperalgesia. This occurs when opioids have the effect of increasing a person's sensitivity to pain instead of reducing it. Ironically, although the patient originally took the drugs to combat chronic pain, those very drugs are partly to blame for the continuation of their pain. Because their baseline experience of pain has been altered, they may be unwilling to stop taking the drugs because they believe the pain will be unbearable.

When those who have become addicted to opioid pain medication are taken off the drugs by their doctors or no longer have legal access to such medications, they often turn to heroin to address their physical dependence. Heroin is more readily available and is often cheaper. Unlike prescription opioids, which come in predefined doses with doctor's instructions, heroin has no set dosage. It is easy for users to increase the amount they take incrementally as they build up a tolerance and because heroin can be injected instead of taken orally, the pain relief—and accompanying euphoria—is achieved more quickly.

To make matters worse, drug dealers often mix heroin with more potent substances as a way to increase potency and reduce costs, thereby increasing their profits. Those who purchase the drugs are often unaware that anything has been added to the heroin. They expect pure heroin and base their dosing on that assumption. The presence of much stronger substances can easily lead to an overdose and, in some cases, death. One of the substances most commonly used as an additive is fentanyl, a synthetic opioid that is 50–100 times more powerful than morphine and 30–50 times more potent than heroin. Although it is used in clinical settings, most of the fentanyl found on the street is produced illicitly. The problem became significant enough that in March of 2015 the US Drug Enforcement Agency issued a nationwide alert about its dangers (U.S. Drug Enforcement Administration, 2015). Until recently, few coroners' offices checked for fentanyl, so its prevalence is probably underreported. Even more problematic is the increasing number of cases involving carfentanil, a fentanyl analog that is up to 100 times more powerful. Unlike fentanyl, carfentanil has no legal medical use in humans. It is primarily used as an elephant tranquilizer. When carfentanil is mixed with heroin, the results are deadly, as seen recently with some high-profile individuals (e.g., Tom Petty and Prince).

Although opioids have grabbed the majority of headlines in recent years, they are not actually the primary drug of choice for people with substance use disorders. That dubious honor continues to be held by alcohol—and not by a small margin. An estimated 15 million adults in the US have an alcohol use disorder. That is 8.4% of the male population and 4.2% of women (National Institute on Alcohol Abuse and Alcoholism, 2021). Roughly 95,000 Americans die from alcohol-related problems each year, making it the third most prevalent cause of preventable deaths. Among working-age adults, one in ten deaths is attributed to excessive alcohol use (Stahre, 2014). Despite—or perhaps because of—its social acceptability, alcohol abuse has a greater negative impact on society than both heroin and cocaine (Nutt, 2010). Despite this, only 6.7% of adults who suffer from alcoholism receive help in any given year (National Institute on Alcohol Abuse and Alcoholism, 2021).

The opioid crisis is continuing to worsen in the United States. In the past two decades, the use of heroin has risen sharply among all demographic groups without regard for gender, ethnicity, age, or income (Centers for Disease Control and Prevention, 2015). As use has increased, the number of deaths from heroin overdoses has risen in tandem, with the number of annual overdose deaths quadrupling from 2010 to 2015 (Centers for Disease Control and Prevention, 2020b). When prescription opioids are included, the numbers are even higher. The Centers for

Disease Control & Prevention report that more than 2 million people in the US abused prescription opioids in 2014 (Centers for Disease Control and Prevention, 2020d).

The use of naloxone, the opioid overdose medication, increased by 400% between 2014 and 2016 (Srivastava, 2018). In 2018, an article in the Mayo Clinic Proceedings identified the need to go beyond providing naloxone. The article, "Beyond Supply: How We Must Tackle the Opioid Epidemic," calls for transformational reforms to the treatment of opioid overdoses:

1. Expanding beyond the narrow administration of overdose reversal to also providing education to physicians on pain and addiction
2. Attention to the prevalence of comorbidity with psychiatric disorders, including suicide
3. Targeted screening of all high-risk patients—or a comprehensive risk assessment if indicated
4. The appropriate use of medication-assisted treatment (MAT)
5. Monitoring strategies with long-term follow-up
6. Contingency management
7. Increased availability of comprehensive psychiatric evaluations
8. Mutual support

"Further, lessons from this epidemic may help us move beyond a specific 'one drug, one approach' so that for future epidemics, irrespective of the drug involved, we would already have in place a generalizable framework that utilizes the full repertoire of responses and resources," wrote the authors, A. Benjamin Srivastava, MD, and Mark S. Gold, MD.

Conclusion

What is lacking at this point is the integration of these disciplines across all treatment settings and coordination between those providing the care. A 2017 study reviewing National Survey of Accountable Care Organizations (NSACO) data revealed only 14% of respondents have nearly complete or fully complete integration of behavioral health and primary care while 43% reported some and another 43% reported no integration of these services.

In 2013, the Agency for Healthcare Research and Quality (AHRQ) made significant strides by publishing the *Lexicon for Behavioral Health and Primary Care Integration: Concepts and Definitions Developed by Expert Consensus*. This report provided how integrated care needs to look and who should support this model, what is the suitable range of patient-centered care services available, identification of those who may benefit most from integrated care, a plan for sharing information in the electronic medical record, and a commitment to quality improvement.

In that same year, the *Lexicon*'s authors brought a group of integration clinicians and researchers together from across the country. They developed the first tool to measure the integration of behavioral health services into primary care settings. This tool, the Practice Integration Profile, was analyzed later that decade by an interdisciplinary group of researchers from medical and behavioral health institutions across the United States. Their research offered a psychometric analysis and a factor analysis of the Practice Integration Profile, with validity and reliability indicators that highlight changes to key domains: Clinical services, workflow, patient engagement, workspace arrangements, integration efforts, and case identification. The Practice Integration Profile is a valuable tool for leaders implementing integrated care.

Despite this progress, the areas of medical and behavioral health have struggled to coordinate, integrate, and collaborate. The two fields continue to be seen as separate forms of healthcare. Medicine has moved toward treating the entirety of the physical person, but the psyche is often not considered. Behavioral health has not helped the situation by its frequent avoidance of MAT and its traditional insistence that it is not part of the healthcare field (Cummings, 2008).

The best healthcare requires treating the person as a whole. Fortunately, from my perspective, doctors have been working to break down the barriers between specialized fields and encourage communication about patient care, especially during the COVID-19 pandemic. I think that this terrible experience has shined a light on the isolation, the lack of socialization, the lack of social support, the increase in anxiety, the fear, the depression, and the loneliness that drives addiction and other behavioral health disorders. I think a greater portion of the public appreciates that a lot of people do not have support structures in place. And I have seen medical doctors' awareness of mental health issues increased even as they learned new digital platforms to interact with their patients.

Efforts have been made to encourage coordination between medical and behavioral fields, but much more needs to be done. The current addiction crisis makes the need for this integrated care even more imperative, as the severity of the crisis calls for it to be addressed from multiple angles. More severe crises are likely to stem from multiple influences, and so need a multidisciplinary team. Furthermore, more severe issues need a level of care that only integrated care can provide.

When measured against the compounded indicators, patients with co-occurring disorders require the greatest efforts and levels of care. It is overwhelming to attempt to master all of the areas required to provide expert care as just diagnosing conditions requires both knowledge and experience. For example, trying to determine whether problems like anxiety or depression are pre-existing disorders separate from substance use disorders or symptoms caused by alcohol or substance use requires a team of professionals. As teams work together throughout a patient's care and complete a differential diagnostic assessment, the chances of identifying and treating multiple needs improve.

Therefore, physical effects, social effects, self-care, and independent functioning, and trauma impacts warrant full professional attention. Physical effects include chronic illnesses, sexually transmitted infections, and blood-borne illnesses. Social effects include loss of family support, poor personal relationships, and victimization issues. Self-care and independent functioning issues include mental illness relapses, malnutrition, unemployment, housing instability, legal issues, and racial discrimination. And trauma impacts include violence, abuse, risk-taking, and sensation-seeking behaviors.

Only integrated care can provide the level of treatment needed to end the crisis.

References

American Psychiatric Association. (2013). *Diagnostic and statistical manual of mental disorders* (5th ed.). Washington DC: Author.

Cadet, J. L., & Gold, M. F. (2017). Methamphetamine-induced psychosis: Who says all drug use is reversible? *Current Psychiatry,* 16(11), 14–20.

Centers for Disease Control and Prevention. (2015). *Today's heroin epidemic.* Retrieved from https://www.cdc.gov/vitalsigns/heroin/

Centers for Disease Control and Prevention. (2018, August 31). *Annual surveillance report of drug-related risks and outcomes – United States.* Retrieved from https://www.cdc.gov/drugoverdose/pdf/pubs/2018-cdc-drug-surveillance-report.pdf

Centers for Disease Control and Prevention. (2020). *CDC guideline for prescribing opioids for chronic pain.* Retrieved from https://www.cdc.gov/mmwr/volumes/65/rr/rr6501e1.htm

Centers for Disease Control and Prevention. (2020). *Heroin overdose data.* Retrieved from https://www.cdc.gov/drugoverdose/data/heroin.html

Centers for Disease Control and Prevention. (2020). *Opioid prescribing.* Retrieved from https://www.cdc.gov/vitalsigns/opioids/

Centers for Disease Control and Prevention. (2020). *Prescription opioid overdose data.* Retrieved from https://www.cdc.gov/drugoverdose/data/overdose.html

Cummings, N. C. (2008). We are not a healthcare business: Our inadvertent vow of poverty. *Journal of Contemporary Psychotherapy.* doi: 10.1007/s10879008909715

Edlund, M. J. (2014). The role of opioid prescription in incident opioid abuse and dependence among individuals with chronic noncancer pain: The role of opioid prescription. *The Clinical Journal of Pain,* 30(7), 557–564. doi: 10.1097/AJP.0000000000000021

Hester, R. K. (1990). In R. C. Ruth, C. Engs (Eds.), *The grand unification theory of alcohol abuse: It's time to stop fighting each other and start working together.* Dubuque, IA: Kendall Hunt.

Kelly, J. F. (2018). E. M. Jellinek's disease concept of alcoholism. *Addiction,* 114, 555–559. doi: 10.1111/add.14400

Magill, J. (2018, October 8). *The liquor capital of America—New Orleans during prohibition*. Retrieved from The Historic New Orleans Collection: https://www.hnoc.org/publications/first-draft/liquor-capital-america%E2%80%94new-orleans-during-prohibition

National Institute of Drug Abuse. (2014, May 14). *America's addiction to opioids: Heroin and prescription drug abuse*. Retrieved from https://archives.drugabuse.gov/testimonies/2014/americas-addiction-to-opioids-heroin-prescription-drug-abuse

National Institute on Alcohol Abuse and Alcoholism. (2021, March). *Alcohol facts and statistics*. Retrieved from https://www.niaaa.nih.gov/alcohol-health/overview-alcohol-consumption/alcohol-facts-and-statistics

Nutt, D. J. (2010). Drug harms in the UK: A multicriteria decision analysis. *Lancet, 376*(9752), 1558–1565. doi: 10.1016/S0140-6736(10)61462-6

O'Donahue, W. T., Cummings, N. A., Cucciare, M. A., Runyan, C. N. and Cummings, J. L. (2006). *Integrated behavioral health care: A guide to effective intervention*. Amherst, NY, US: Humanity Books.

Okrent, D. (2010). *Last call: The rise and fall of Prohibition (1st Scribner hardcover ed.)*. New York, NY: Scribner.

Sites, B. D. (2014). Increases in the use of prescription opioid analgesics and the lack of improvement in disability metrics among users. *Regional Anesthesia and Pain Medicine, 39*(1), 6–12. doi: 10.1097/AAP.000000

Srivastava, A. B. (2018). Beyond supply: How we must tackle the opioid epidemic. *Mayo Clinic Proceedings, 93*(3), 269–272.

Stahre, M., Roeber, J., Kanny, D., Brewer, R., and Zhang, X. (2014). Contribution of excessive alcohol consumption to deaths and years of potential life lost in the United States. *Preventing Chronic Disease, 11*, E109, 10.5888/pcd11.130293.

U.S. Drug Enforcement Administration. (2015, March 18). *DEA issues nationwide alert on fentanyl as threat to health and public safety*. Retrieved from https://www.dea.gov/divisions/hq/2015/hq031815.shtml

White, W. L. (2014). *Slaying the dragon: The history of addiction treatment and recovery in America* (2nd ed.). Bloomington, IL: Chestnut Health System/Lighthouse Institute.

Wilson, B. (1957). *Alcoholics Anonymous comes of age: A brief history of A. A.* (1st ed.). New York: Alcoholics Anonymous Pub.

3 Overcoming Barriers

At River Oaks, I practiced on the Masters and Johnson Trauma/Compulsivity Programs, leading the behavior therapy, the extended care program, and the research programs. After 13 years of working with this avant-garde approach, the investment that had been gifted to me would pay dividends.

I was presented with the opportunity to bring some of these ideas to a willing, but nascent, organization. I was approached by a large behavioral health and addiction treatment center. At the time, Pine Grove Behavioral Health and Addiction Services in Hattiesburg, Mississippi, was known for its traditional, standard yet effective approach to addiction care. The CEO, however, thought something different and innovative was needed.

The late Vicki Pevsner, CEO was a trained social worker who had completed her internship at the Yale School of Medicine's Child Study Center which meant that she wanted a quality product driven by high caliber professionals. She was a visionary who often gathered some of the brightest and best clinicians from across the United States. Her work ethic was driven by grand ideas which she led others to strategically execute.

Fortunately, Mrs. Pevsner was open to new ideas and wanted someone to implement a new collaborative approach. She pointed out that they had the resources, facilities, and talent but wanted to know if I would be interested in designing programs using their professional teams. A prolonged visit to the center convinced me that this was a chance to put into practice the concepts that had become foundational to my understanding of mental healthcare and addiction.

I jumped at the chance. It was the start of a career trajectory that would extend the work begun at River Oaks into the future. As the director of the Professional Enhancement Program, I was able to begin integrating models of care, psychological theories, and innovative treatment interventions—all customized to treat professional and other healthcare provider population.

DOI: 10.4324/9781003128571-3

I partnered with Alexis Polles, MD and other existing professional staff and then recruited and trained talented, eager clinicians. The model evolved as I began spreading the philosophy and clinical approaches of integrated care while reinforcing how it relates to personality and addiction treatment. I was able to develop a collaborative multidisciplinary team that was led by a dynamic medical staff and could address all aspects of a patient's life. We evaluated the clients across a broad spectrum of factors that influenced mental health. We sought to understand the entirety of their condition so that we could focus on the entirety of their recovery.

Of course, we faced barriers at Pine Grove with the acceptance of this new, different approach to care. Some professional staff refused to participate in conjoint training or marketing efforts or would not make internal referrals. Others struggled to exercise agility as new team members were recruited. There are always major barriers in healthcare, especially when the change you want to make is transformative. But one critical element we had was buy-in.

The First Hurdle

Getting that understanding and commitment from the CEO was a critical foundation for Pine Grove's success. One of the universal rules I have experienced in my three decades of working with centers to move them toward integrated care is this: Unless people at all levels of an organization are convinced of the value of integrated care, it is difficult—if not impossible—to achieve full integration.

Without buy-in from management, care providers, referral sources, and support staff, the task of integrating medical and behavioral healthcare faces an insurmountable barrier. In my experience, the most crucial buy-in of all is leadership and Primary Care Providers (PCPs).

The role of the PCP as a team leader is important on several levels. Chronologically, their first leadership role takes the form of buy-in to the integrated health model. For a collaborative care model to work, the PCP must be fully on board. The PCP's willingness—or lack thereof—to embrace the system can make or break attempts to integrated care. PCPs are often concerned that integrated care will add to their workload or that it will reduce the already limited amount of time they are able to spend with each patient. Some feel protective of their turf and do not want to share their space. In such cases, integrated care has little chance of taking root.

Once PCPs are convinced that integrated care is a better way of practicing medicine and see that it actually reduces their workload and increases the time they can spend with patients who need their attention, their leadership is invaluable. Their enthusiasm infects the rest of the staff, creating an environment where coordination and collaboration can thrive. Their buy-in also affects how patients respond to integrated behavioral health because PCPs have usually developed a relationship of trust with their clients. Patients are more open to integrated care when they know their doctor believes in it as well.

The more people who view the model as one that provides the best outcomes, the easier the process becomes and the more funding becomes available. For that reason, this book includes two whole chapters dedicated to making the case for integrated care. Feel free to reference that chapter for staff presentations, grant applications, and other opportunities where persuasion of the benefits of integrated care is a key tactic for putting an implementation in place.

Buy-in is one of the most common and crucial barriers, but it is not the only one. The rest of this chapter is devoted to going through the key barriers, one by one, and illustrating the tools I have used to overcome them.

Systemic Hurdles

While each field of healthcare has its own shortcomings, one problem that can affect all of us is a lack of communication. This is actually the number one cause of errors within patient care. Patients can visit several specialists without the other specialists being aware of it unless the patient informs them.

You will have to overcome deeply ingrained communication issues: Providers and other stakeholders often lack the habit of communicating and the intention to communicate. What is more, the brilliant minds of our industry often lack basic interpersonal communication skills.

Even when communication among practitioners within one organization is present, sharing of information between practices can be problematic. The advent of internet-enabled EHR systems has alleviated some of the technical problems associated with such communication, but true coordination of care still requires intentionality on the part of doctors, particularly PCPs. When they do share information, it is further complicated by the security requirements of the Health Insurance Portability and Accountability Act (HIPAA) and the incompatibility of different EHR systems.

And finally, there are the payment barriers. Insurance coverage drives much of the decision-making in clinical settings, and a lack of buy-in from insurance companies can cut integrated care off at the knees. Many healthcare leaders view this issue as largely out of their control. But there are strategies to improve the profitability of integrated care—starting with cost savings generated by the implementation of the model itself. Starting with a care coordinator or case manager, send a message to the insurance companies and organizations that you are serious about your commitment.

The larger problem is the direct communication between the fields of medicine and behavioral health. Although each group has made strides in sharing information and coordinating care within their fields, barriers remain (University of Washington, Psychiatry & Behavioral Sciences Division of Population Health, 2021). This is due in large part to the fact that the fields are still seen as unrelated disciplines by patients despite the expansion of telehealth resulting in increased access to mental health services. Physical health is often considered unrelated to mental health and vice versa. Many healthcare professionals do recognize that they are part of the same continuum. When medical professionals are alerted to psychological conditions, SUD, and behavioral health struggles, they can actually serve as one of the biggest barriers to their patients being addressed in a holistic manner.

I believe this results from issues within the culture of medicine. There are always late adopters to innovative technology. Physicians, on the whole, are laggards to adopting the relatively new fields such as behavioral health—and especially to the broader suite of biopsychosocial and spiritual tactics that we as BHPs have embraced from other fields. I am thinking of sleep hygiene, mindfulness, and other evidence-based solutions that lie outside the realm of pharmaceuticals.

For physicians in primary care and the various somatic specialties to succeed within the integrated care model, they must transcend this cultural barrier. They must embrace a commitment to treatment that addresses the person as a whole, which necessitates viewing the behavioral and medical fields as part of a larger blended model. Both contribute to the overall health of the individual; therefore, they are working toward the same goal, usually from different locations when communication is available.

The social sciences have generally done a better job of addressing the entirety of the individual. Social work, in particular, embraces collaboration with other fields to understand humans from a holistic perspective that incorporates all aspects of human existence. Although different practitioners may approach humanity from different theoretical perspectives within a particular field (for example, Freudian versus behavioral models in psychology), social workers are trained to incorporate knowledge from multiple fields in their quest for understanding.

Conclusion

The benefits of integrated care are many. Lower costs and improved outcomes number among them. And we saw those kinds of results at Pine Grove.

During my 12 years there, 1,500 doctors and other health professionals traveled from 48 states and three foreign countries for treatment. But the job hit, quite literally, close to home when we provided educational and supportive services to over 1,000 legal, mental health, and medical professionals in the wake of hurricanes Katrina and Rita. That is when I experienced my greatest return—in providing a high quality of care to people who do so much good for their communities.

Success, however, can only be achieved with substantial communication among all health practitioners. Communication allows for the integration of care, which leads to better patient outcomes. Whether across the halls of a clinic or through a virtual provider workshop, medical and behavioral health providers have to come together—for the sake of the patient.

Reference

University of Washington, Psychiatry & Behavioral Sciences Division of Population Health. (2021). *AIMS center: Advancing integrated mental health solutions*. Retrieved from University of Washington: https://aims.uw.edu/.

4 Making the Ethical Case

Imagine that you have just inherited a house from a relative. The house appears to be in poor condition, so you decide to hire some people to fix it up. The most obvious problem is the appearance of the interior, so you hire a painting company to give every room in the house a fresh coat of paint. When they are finished, it looks great, but about a week later a small fire breaks out. It is quickly contained, but most of the rooms suffer damage from the smoke.

The fire marshal determines that the fire was caused by faulty wiring, and an inspection of the wiring indicates that it all needs to be replaced. So, you hire an electrician to rip out all the old wiring and replace it with a system that is up to code. When they are finished, however, many of the walls have been cut to install the new wiring. You have to hire more people to repair the sheetrock and plaster. Then, to take care of damage caused by both the wiring repair and the fire, the painters have to come back to repaint the walls.

Unfortunately, a rainstorm the following month reveals that the roof is in bad shape. Water is leaking through the roof, ruining portions of the interior. You are forced to call in a roofer to assess the needs. After they complete the process of shingling the roof, you have to ask the contractors to return to fix the water damage to the walls, followed by another call to the painters.

A few months later, you notice cracks in the walls. It turns out that problems with the foundation are causing the house to shift. Once again, you begin a series of calls, this time to various sub-contractors and construction companies.

The problem with your approach to repairing the house had nothing to do with the people you hired. Each of them knew their craft well and did a good job. The problem was with the person you did not hire: A general contractor. If you had engaged the services of a general contractor at the very beginning, they could have assessed the overall condition of the house. They would have brought in an inspector, who would have recommended an assessment by a structural engineer. The problems with

DOI: 10.4324/9781003128571-4

the foundation, the roof, and the wiring would have been discovered before you started the repairs.

The contractor would have been able to not only identify the problems but also to determine the order in which they needed to be fixed. The foundation would have been repaired first. The roof and the wiring could have been fixed concurrently, and the painters would only be called in after all the other work had been done. This process is more efficient, avoids the need for multiple visits by the painters, and allows problems like the fire to be entirely averted—and greatly decreases costs.

Medical care works in a similar way. Going to the right specialists allows you to be treated for specific problems. But when one person, such as a primary care physician, is coordinating the care, the overall level of healthcare is improved. The right treatments can be administered at the right time and in the right order to bring about the best results. In the past few decades, the medical field has made some progress toward integrating care and increasing communication between specialists in somatic medicine.

However, the integration of behavioral health with medical care is not as far along. Often, medical and behavioral health still function in separate areas. Primary care physicians may refer their patients to behavioral health services for depression, anxiety, addiction, or other problems, but the handoff is seen as the final step in the process. Minimal to no communication process is established between the PCP and the behavioral therapist that would allow for the coordination of care. Steps have been taken to overcome this problem, but a lot more needs to be done.

Integrated care—especially collaboration between medical and behavioral health—is a superior, gold standard method for helping patients achieve and maintain physical and mental well-being (Agency for Healthcare Research and Quality, n.d.). This chapter is here to help those who need to convince others of the value of integrated care.

The ethical case for integrated care can be given in one sentence: Integrated care provides better outcomes and improves access.

Yes, you can make the case in one sentence. But you do not have to stop there. That is because integrated care also addresses all the issues contributing to illness and disorder, making it a more effective approach. It allows earlier diagnosis when treatment is generally more effective. Integrated care empowers patients in a healthcare system that makes them feel a lack of control. It reduces churn and burnout among healthcare employees.

And finally, it reduces healthcare disparities. When I started writing this book, I considered health disparities an unspoken reality. Fortunately, that has changed somewhat during the Black Lives Matter movement. Cultural and racial discrimination may add to an individual's struggle to feel trust, safety, and/or engagement. More people are speaking about these issues now. But disparities are still the reality, and integrated care can help.

One of the goals of integrated treatment is improving care, but it also reduces health disparities in care. If a person is able to get a number of their needs met in one place and one coordinated effort, then that cuts down on the number of transitions. This cuts down on opportunities for discrimination in the healthcare setting—or for reliving past experiences of discrimination simply by having to navigate a new setting and be open to the possibility that it will happen again. That vulnerability increases the already high likelihood that someone will not show up for a scheduled appointment with a new provider.

While my work has been limited to the systems I have engaged with, I believe that collaborative care improves access for racial and ethnic minority groups, addresses gender and ageism bias by including multiple providers on the team, lowers the cost while maintaining standards of care, and ultimately fosters job satisfaction and cohesion for healthcare workers.

I found tremendous need and success within the application of this model to the adolescent population with systems of care as well when I was employed by various group homes and state-funded institutions. Not only did the patients and their families respond well to this whole care, but the staff did as well. The dynamic model being deployed infused them with enthusiasm. For most professional clinicians, this was the amalgam of care they had spent years studying. Both patients and staff sustained a high level of engagement, which offered a parallel growth arc for providers. This growth also occurred among interfacing schools and judicial settings, which were very responsive to the team-based care as they pivoted to this model as well.

The goal of the process is to increase patients' access to both medical and behavioral care, while also developing their health literacy. The delivery of team-based behavioral health and primary care ensures that the whole person is treated and all aspects of health are addressed.

The experts are in agreement on the need for integrated care. In 2015, the American College of Physicians (ACP) highlighted the importance of this need. The ACP supports the integration of behavioral healthcare into primary care and encourages its members to address behavioral health issues within the limits of their competencies and resources, according to The Integration of Care for Mental Health, Substance Abuse, and Other Behavioral Health Conditions into Primary Care.

According to the National Institute of Mental Health (NIMH), three major factors within healthcare make integrated behavioral and medical healthcare a necessity. These are:

- Primary care settings, like a doctor's office, provide about half of all mental healthcare for common psychiatric disorders
- Adults with serious mental illnesses and substance use disorders also have higher rates of chronic physical illnesses and die earlier than the general population

- People with common physical health conditions also have higher rates of mental health issues

Additionally, consider both "Facing Addiction in America" and "Facing addiction in America: The Surgeon General's Spotlight on Opioids" report on drug and alcohol abuse published in (United States Preventive Services Task Force, 2016) and respectively. The reports note the need for addiction-related healthcare to be the responsibility not just of specialized treatment centers but of general practitioners as well. They call for the integration of addiction treatment into mainstream medicine with personalized diagnosis, as well as assessment and treatment plans that improve individuals' productivity, health, and overall quality of life. This commitment to long-term disease management includes FDA-approved medications and recovery support services. The risk of not adopting integration is obsolescence and not incorporating best practices.

In 2019, the NAATP released their guide to the core competencies for treatment providers to follow (National Association of Addiction Treatment Providers, 2019) as a product of their Quality Assurance Initiative, which identified the following organizational values:

- The history of significant contributions made by 12-step abstinence-based treatment to the sobriety of over 20 million Americans in recovery
- Residential treatment's vital, necessary, and essential place in the full continuum of care as a viable choice for the treatment of the disease of addiction
- A comprehensive model of care that addresses the medical, biopsychosocial, and spiritual needs of individuals and families impacted by the disease of addiction
- Outcome data that inform the efficacy of treatment interventions
- Education and training that promotes understanding of a continuum of care that embraces these values
- Depending on biopsychosocial and economic factors, there may be persons who might require medication-assisted treatment for extended periods of time and perhaps indefinitely. However, medication alone is usually not sufficient to maintain long-term recovery.
- Research-driven, evidence-based treatment interventions that integrate the sciences of medicine, therapy, and spirituality:
    - Pharmaceutical interventions, including medications for reducing craving and withdrawal symptoms
    - Psychosocial interventions, including cognitive-behavioral therapy which assist in the identification of cognitions that lead to behaviors, and motivational interviewing which focused on the patient's lead to change

- Spiritual interventions, including 12 step-facilitated therapy and mindfulness meditation
- Behavioral interventions, including nutrition and exercise

Coordinated Care as Best Practice

As care providers, we have an ethical obligation to ensure that our patients are receiving the most effective and efficacious treatment available. This is expressed in one of the four foundational principles of medical ethics: Beneficence.

This obligation is especially important for serious conditions, where substandard care can have lasting effects. Both acute and chronic ailments can lead to severely reduced quality of life, loss of abilities and functionality, and even death if not treated properly. Integrated care leads to better outcomes in both mental and physical health, in addition to improved overall well-being.

The costs and benefits of programs like these are often difficult to quantify. This is due, in part, to the fact that the savings are often spread across a number of years and are realized in a number of ways. For example, a smoking program's monetary impact must take into account not only the health of the individual who chooses not to take up smoking but also peripheral effects. Not taking up smoking usually means better health for the patient, which in turn leads to them engaging in a lower level of healthcare utilization, thereby putting less of a burden on the system. Integrated care provides treatment sooner, lowering long-term costs, but also creating a net benefit to society through the lower utilization of treatment facilities/care providers, less lost time at work, and even decreased danger to others from secondhand smoke. Quality of life is also increased but may be hard to quantify.

A growing body of evidence supports the idea of integrated care as a best practice in behavioral health (Raney, 2017a). For mental health, the efficacy of integrated care in treaing conditions such as anxiety, depression, and post-traumatic stress disorders is well-established (Garrity, 2016). Integrated care allows for earlier diagnosis of disease states, which allows these conditions to be treated before they become serious problems.

When problems are detected earlier, the patient can get treatment sooner, possibly avoiding the complications that arise once the issues become acute. For the patient, this means better outcomes, fewer disruptions to their lives, and lower out-of-pocket costs.

Because it is so prevalent, depression is an area where the effects of integrated care can be easily seen. About 6.7% of adults in the US suffers from major depressive disorder, while an additional 1.5% is dealing with persistent depressive disorder (Anxiety and Depression Association of America, 2021). Screening by PCPs allows depression to be diagnosed sooner and treated at earlier stages. When depression is treated through integrated care, the results are greatly improved over treatments that do not involve a behavioral care specialist (Coventry, 2014). Treatment of depression within a care setting that integrates both PCPs and Behavioral Health Providers contributes to earlier diagnosis, shorter wait times, and treatment results with fewer sessions (Hser, 2017).

This disease stretches across the life span, so pediatricians are recommended to provide annual screenings for 12–18-year-old patients (United States Preventive Services Task Force, 2016). The improved outcomes that result also extend to post-partum depression, which has been shown to be better treated by collaborative care than non-integrated practices (Truitt, 2013). The recent assignment of priority and breakthrough therapy status by the FDA and ultimately approval of Zulresso, the first treatment for post-partum depression, indicates the power of crossing practice silos of obstetrics and psychiatry that will finally allow women to receive state-of-the-art treatment (Food and Drug Administration, 2019).

An even more common mental health problem is anxiety, which affects 18.1% of adults in the US (Anxiety and Depression Association of America, 2021). Although studies of the effectiveness of collaborative care are few in number, those that are present suggest it improves outcomes (Muntingh, 2017). The integration of a behavioral health provider into a primary practice setting has also been shown to lead to better outcomes for patients whose anxiety is insufficiently treated by medication (Campbell-Sills, 2016). Other conditions, such as bipolar disorder and schizophrenia, also show improved outcomes with collaborative care (O'Neill, 2017).

The data on the effectiveness of collaborative care in treating substance use disorders is promising but as of yet inconclusive (Raney, 2017b). The evidence is not as well-established, but the data that are present suggest integrated care is an effective mode of treatment in need of more research studies (Watkins, 2017). The Substance Abuse and Mental Health Services Administration (SAMHSA) has been encouraging the use of Screening, Brief Intervention, and Referral to Treatment (SBIRT) as a way to detect emerging substance use disorders (Substance Abuse and Mental Health Services Administration, 2017). Reviews of SBIRT programs have shown that they lead to small reductions in alcohol consumption among moderate drinkers and decreased numbers of alcohol-related emergency room repeat visits (Barata, 2017).

Integrated care means that providers are working toward the same goals and the appropriate specialists are addressing all the problems. It allows the person to be treated in a holistic/comprehensive manner, which has seen increased acceptance and creative implementation by many providers.

Physical Health Outcomes

The benefits of integrated care within physical medicine are well documented. When multiple specialties collaborate on treatment, improvements in treatment outcomes are often seen. In addition, integrated care leads to patients making fewer doctor and hospital visits, thereby cutting down on the overall usage of the system. This not only conserves medical resources, making them available to more patients but also reduces the cost for individual patients.

The improved outcomes with integrated care can also be seen when behavioral healthcare is incorporated into physical healthcare. Although it may seem obvious that integrating behavioral health into primary care will result in better mental health outcomes, what may not be obvious is that such integrated care also leads to improvement in physical health. But as many doctors will tell you, the strong connection between the body and mind means that what happens in the brain affects our physical health as well.

One study supporting this conclusion examined patients presenting in primary care with somatic symptoms (Kroenke, 2003). Approximately one-third of these symptoms appeared to have no medical cause. The study showed that patients presenting with unexplained physical symptoms often had anxiety disorders, depression, and other mental health issues. Addressing these psychological issues often led to the reduction or elimination of the somatic problems. Incorporating behavioral health into primary care can, therefore, lead to better physical outcomes.

Patients who have good mental health are also better equipped to face accidents or illnesses and the subsequent recovery. For example, patients who have had heart attacks are 20% more likely than the general population to suffer from depression (Schroeder, 2016). That depression affects their recovery. Patients who are depressed are less likely to take their medications on time, eat healthy foods, and engage in other activities that contribute to the recovery. In addition, patients who received treatment for depression were more likely to survive a subsequent heart attack than those whose depression went untreated (Zuidersma, 2013).

That same relationship between physical and mental health has also been found in other diseases. People who have a mental illness are 30% more likely to die if they develop cancer than people without psychiatric issues (Kisely, 2013). One reason for this may be the fact that they seek treatment for cancer later than people without mental health problems (Clifton, 2016). An integrated approach to cancer screening can allow cancer to be detected earlier, bringing about parity in treatment between people with and without mental illnesses.

The improved physical and mental health that comes from integrated care also results in a better overall well-being. This is due to the intimate connection between the mind and body. Improvements in one area can create a positive feedback loop that leads to better health. People who are in better physical health tend to exercise more, which can help fight depression. Patients who are less depressed then feel more like exercising. Fewer somatic problems can lead to a reduction in stress and anxiety, which in turn means fewer physical manifestations of mental problems.

Increased Access

The second prong of the ethical argument for integrated care is access. The cost of healthcare has been rising dramatically in recent decades. The Affordable Care Act addressed some of the problems and may have slowed the growth in costs, but many problems still remain. Integrated care means conditions are diagnosed and treated sooner, which leads to better outcomes and aids in controlling the costs of treatment.

Cost, of course, is a business concern, but it is also an ethical concern because the out-of-pocket cost is a major factor in access to healthcare. It does not matter how effective a treatment approach is if people cannot afford the treatment in the first place. From an ethical standpoint, therefore, an approach that lowers the costs while maintaining the standard of care is a good thing.

The financial impact of integrated care on a medical practice can be measured in two ways: Cost-effectiveness (CE) and return on investment (ROI). CE requires fully understanding all components of what a program produces and the targeted population being served. This provides the outcomes and potential benefits for necessary conversations with funding sources. The results of implementing integrated care have been reported by a number of medical and behavioral health organizations and by health insurance providers. The data show a substantial reduction in medical costs as well as an increased ROI (Children's Health Alliance of Wisconsin, 2017).

Collaborative care has been shown to be a cost-effective treatment approach to a number of conditions related to both physical and mental health (Unützer, 2008). Treating a disease in its early stages costs less than waiting until the disease is in later stages or additional complications have developed. Integrated care also makes treatment more efficient, resulting in shorter treatment times and decreased use of medical resources (Bertakis, 2011). While the data are not yet conclusive with regard to all medical conditions (Grochtdreis, 2015), in general, they suggest that integrated care increases CE across the spectrum.

The ability of integrated care to decrease expenditures can be seen in several examples. A New Mexico study documented cost savings in the treatment of cardiovascular diseases, reporting savings of over two million dollars over two years (Awa, Plaumann, and Walter, 2010). The Denver Health Community Health Worker Program implemented care coordination for patients in underserved populations with chronic diseases, which led to a savings of almost $96,000 annually to the insurance company (Whitley, 2006). The same lowering of costs is observed in mental health settings. The Intermountain Healthcare Mental Health Integration Program lowered costs by $670 compared to patients not receiving integrated care, while the IMPACT program (Improving Mood—Promoting Access to Collaborative Treatment) yielded savings across the board when implemented in five states (Reiss-Brennan, 2010). In the same way, SBIRT in Wisconsin resulted in a savings of $782 per patient over a two-year period (Paltzer, 2017).

Lower costs are directly beneficial to patients when it decreases the costs they pay out of pocket. But integrated care helps patients even when—or perhaps especially when—they do not directly pay for treatment themselves. When medical costs are contained, insurers pay less for individual procedures and programs. With this happening across the spectrum, insurers have more money available to pay for better treatment approaches, higher quality care systems, and more advanced interventions in general.

This increases the amount of healthcare available to people. This not only improves outcomes for individuals but also leads to an overall healthier population, which in turn means fewer healthcare visits, further lowering the costs.

Let us go back to our imaginary exercise in renovating the house. Because you hired a contractor to help all the subcontractors communicate, you cut significantly into your expenditures on building materials and labor.

It is as if the price of the shingles, drywall, lumber, and wiring magically dropped—by a significant amount. Now, you face a much lower barrier to doing much more remodeling around your property. You can now create the house of your dreams.

Hence, the power of integration.

References

Agency for Healthcare Research and Quality. (n.d.). *The academy*. Retrieved from https://integrationacademy.ahrq.gov/

Anxiety and Depression Association of America. (2021, February 2). *Facts & statistics*. Retrieved from https://adaa.org/about-adaa/press-room/facts-statistics

Awa, W. L., Plaumann, M., & Walter, U. (2010). Burnout prevention: A review of intervention programs. *Patient Education and Counseling, 78*(2), 184–190.

Barata, I. A. K. (2017). Effectiveness of SBIRT for alcohol use disorders in the emergency department: A systematic review. *Western Journal of Emergency Medicine, 18*(6), 1143.

Bertakis, K. D. (2011). Patient-centered care is associated with decreased health care utilization. *Journal of American Board Family Medicine, 24*(3), 229–239. doi: 10.3122/jabfm.2011.03.100170

Campbell-Sills, L. R. B. (2016). Improving outcomes for patients with medication-resistant anxiety: Effects of collaborative care with cognitive behavioral therapy. *Depression and Anxiety*, *33*(12), 1099–1106.

Children's Health Alliance of Wisconsin. (2017, March 13). *Initial business case for coordinated team-based care*. Retrieved from https://cdn.ymaws.com/www.wpha.org/resource/resmgr/legislative/Prevention_services_business.pdf

Clifton, A. B. (2016). Influences on uptake of cancer screening in mental health service users: A qualitative study. *BMC Health Services Research*, *16*(1), 257. doi: 10.1186/s12913-016-1505-04

Coventry, P. H. (2014). Characteristics of effective collaborative care for treatment of depression: A systematic review and meta-regression of 74 randomised controlled trials. *PLoS One*, *9*(9), e108114–e108114 doi: 10.1371/journal.pone.0108114

Food and Drug Administration. (2019, March 19). *FDA approves first treatment for post-partum depression*. Retrieved from https://www.fda.gov/news-events/press-announcements/fda-approves-first-treatment-post-partum-depression

Garrity, M. (2016). *Evolving models of behavioral health integration: Evidence update 2010–2015*. Milbank Memorial Fund. (Accessed August 8, 2021) https://www.milbank.org/wp-content/uploads/2016/05/Evolving-Models-of-BHI.pdf

Grochtdreis, T. B.-H. (2015). Cost-effectiveness of collaborative care for the treatment of depressive disorders in primary care: A systematic review. *PLOS One*, *10*(5), e0123078–e0123078. doi: 10.1371/journal.pone.0123078

Hser, Y. J. (2017). High mortality among patients with opioid use disorder in a large healthcare system. *Journal of Addiction Medicine*, *11*(4), 315–319.

Kisely, S. C. (2013). Cancer-related mortality in people with mental illness. *Journal of the American Medical Association: Psychiatry*, *70*(2), 209–217. doi: 10.1001/jamapsychiatry.2013.278.

Kroenke, K. (2003). Patients presenting with somatic complaints: Epidemiology, psychiatric co-morbidity and management. *International Journal of Methods in Psychiatric Research*, *12*(1), 34–43.

Muntingh, A. D.-C. (2017). Collaborative care for anxiety disorders in primary. *BMC Family Practice*, 17(1), 1–15. doi: 10.1186/s12875-016-0466-3

National Association of Addiction Treatment Providers. (2019, April). *The Addiction treatment provider quality assurance guidebook: A guide to the core competencies for the delivery of addiction treatment services*. Retrieved from https://www.naatp.org/sites/naatp.org/files/NAATP%20QA%20Guidebook%20Beta.pdf

O'Neill, E. A. (2017). Collaborative care for individuals with bipolar disorder or schizophrenia and co-occurring physical health conditions: A systematic review. *Social Work in Mental Health*, *15*(6), 705–729.

Paltzer, J. B. (2017). Substance use screening, brief intervention, and referral to treatment among Medicaid patients in Wisconsin: Impacts on healthcare utilization and costs. *The Journal of Behavioral Health Services & Research*, *44*(1), 102–112.

Raney, L. E. (2017). Elements of effective design and implementation. In L. E. Raney, *Integrated care: A guide for effective implementation* (pp. 7–8). Arlington, VA: APA Publishing.

Raney, L. E. (2017). *Integrated care: A guide for effective implementation*. Washington, DC: American Psychiatric Association Publishing.

Reiss-Brennan, B. B. (2010). Cost and quality impact of Intermountain's mental health integration program. *Journal of Healthcare Management, 55*(2), 97.

Schroeder, M. O. (2016, February 25). *Depression can threaten recovery after a heart attack*. Retrieved from https://health.usnews.com/health-news/patient-advice/articles/2016-02-25/depression-can-threaten-recovery-after-a-heart-attack

Substance Abuse and Mental Health Services Administration. (2017, September 15). *Screening, brief intervention, and referral to treatment (SBIRT)*. Retrieved from Substance Abuse and Mental Health Services Administration: https://www.samhsa.gov/sbirt

Truitt, F. P.-R. (2013). Outcomes for collaborative care versus routine care in the management of postpartum depression. *Quality in Primary Care, 21*, 171–177.

United States Preventive Services Task Force. (2016, February 8). *Final recommendation statement: Depression in children and adolescents: Screening*. Retrieved from https://www.uspreventiveservicestaskforce.org/uspstf/document/RecommendationStatementFinal/depression-in-

Unützer, J. K. (2008). Long-term cost effects of collaborative care for late-life depression. *The American Journal of Managed Care, 14*(2), 95.

Watkins, K. E. (2017). Collaborative care for opioid and alcohol use disorders in primary care: The SUMMIT randomized clinical trial. *Journal of the American Medical Association: Internal Medicine, 177*(10), 1480–1488. doi: 10.1001/jamainternmed.2017.3947

Whitley, E. M. (2006). Measuring return on investment of outreach by community health workers. *Journal of Health Care for the Poor and Underserved, 17*(1), 6–15.

Zuidersma, M. C. (2013). Depression treatment after myocardial infarction and long-term risk of subsequent cardiovascular events and mortality: A randomized controlled trial. *Journal of Psychosomatic Research, 74*(1), 25–30.

5 Making the Business Case

While the ethical case for integrated care is a strong one, that argument can be supplemented with a business case. Although we would like to think that healthcare is an altruistic field where people are motivated only by a desire to help others, we know that is not the case.

While medical and behavioral health can be micro, mezzo, and macro-human service organizations that focus on care delivery systems for the "whole person," they are tasked with improving this care, optimizing care cost, and improving overall population health. The impact and effectiveness of this triple aim approach can be seen in the Partners in Recovery model, which aims to support people with severe and persistent mental illness with complex needs and their care providers and families, by getting multiple sectors, services, and supports they may come into contact with (and could benefit from) to work in a more collaborative, coordinated, and integrated way (COPA Health, 2020).

This model has demonstrated integration with serious mental illness (SMI) by addressing "whole-person health, wellness, and social inclusion." In 2017, Partners in Recovery improved outcomes among the SMI population which included offering people increased access to primary care visits by 33%, reducing psychiatric hospital admissions by 29%, increasing competitive employment by 73%, and reducing emergency department visits by 29%. The focus on suicide prevention became a "one-stop shop" model to address these needs which were previously ignored. Cross-portfolio and cross-government collaboration was needed to develop these systems, structures, and co-design strategies that are committed to the shared responsibility of those in need. Partners in Recovery took ineffective, fragmented, and unintegrated care and managed it much more effectively. For example, primary care and psychiatry in the same suite allow sharing of electronic health records (EHR) which eliminates the lack of interoperability, standing in-vivo consultations, weekly cross-specialty staffing meetings, primary care physician (PCP), and care coordinator collaborations, increased response times, and wellness engagement.

44 *Making the Business Case*

This model provides not only sound clinical care but also business best practices, which we will ignore at our peril. So, fortunately, the business case for integrated care is just as compelling as the ethical arguments.

On the business side, the arguments include increased profitability, greater engagement by employees, and integration with the community. This chapter explores each of these in turn as a way to bolster the case for integrated care.

The Bottom Line

Focusing on ways in which integrated care can increase profitability and control costs only strengthens its relevance. Business growth is necessary to consider as well-cared-for patients become ambassadors for medical providers and integrated care increases community involvement and engagement, thereby creating goodwill within the community. Finally, the benefits accrue within organizations as employee engagement grows, leading to a more satisfied workforce, lower turnover and burnout rates, and a healthier corporate environment.

Successful patients increase profitability. People prefer to be treated at centers that have a positive record of accomplishment. As has been shown above, integrated care leads to better outcomes, which in turn contributes to profitability. In addition, well-cared-for patients become spokespeople for the business, and word of mouth is the best free advertising.

The patient is the most important component of integrated care. This statement may seem like a redundancy. After all, without the patient, there would be no need for treatment. Yet the meaning of this statement goes beyond that.

Under standard models of care, patients are often seen to be consumers. They pay for and consume a service from medical care providers. They receive care in a passive way, much in the same way that someone would have the oil in their car changed or the tiles in their kitchen replaced. They have a small role—choosing the grade of oil or deciding on a style of tile—but the work is done by others, which is a very Western approach.

In integrated care, however, the patients are a central part of the care team. Integrated care is intended not only to provide better care but also to empower patients to make decisions and take responsibility for their own health. This is true for both medical and behavioral health issues. It is, therefore, imperative that the role of the patient as a component of integrated care be considered.

The Agency for Healthcare Research and Quality under the US Department of Health and Human Services examined the practices of eight high-performing primary care organizations that included integrated behavioral health. Researchers conducted site visits that included observation and interviews. This methodology allowed them to identify those practices that contributed to the successful coordination of care. Their results were published as A Guidebook of Professional Practices for Behavioral Health and Primary Care Integration (Cohen, 2015). AHRQ's guidebook for integrated care is a great resource, including the tactics for good communication with the patients. The guidebook says that communication with patients is always crucial. It recommends that clinicians should employ multiple modes of communication, including phone calls, hallway consultations in vivo, secure email, patient portals, and in-person visits. And finally, the guidebook notes that unnecessary visits to the clinic should be avoided, both to prevent inconveniencing the patient and to alleviate overloaded schedules for the staff.

Because integrated care involves better patient engagement and education, closer integration with the community is required for implementation. This naturally increases the health center's visibility while leading to greater goodwill among people in the area. This seamless membership of the community is the best version of what marketers refer to as staying "top of mind."

When these community members are later in need of healthcare, they will be more likely to turn to a center with which they already have a connection, feel a trusting relationship, and anticipate safety. This community confidence can therefore lead to a larger patient base.

Human service organizations and institutions were once cornerstones that were fixtures and were an integral component of everyone's life cycle. Integrated care can help your practice regain that role.

Relationships are powerful fuel for profitability, both at a community level and at a one-to-one level with patients. If you have very strong communication and rapport with your patient, even if there is an adverse outcome, your rapport may be able to survive that negative situation, and the healing can continue. The rapport may even be so powerful that it reduces liability for providers. In other words, if a patient feels like you were genuine in your interactions, and if you really connected, they are actually less likely to sue you. This has happened with people who made even egregious mistakes, such as operating on the wrong side of the body. Feeling truly cared for is so powerful, that it resolves people's sense of powerlessness and, as a result, disarms their hostility.

ROI is also improved when integrated care is put in place, as value-based care has improved accountability. For example, a substance abuse treatment program in Wisconsin saw a $3.20 return for every dollar invested in the Project TrEAT (Trial for Early Alcohol Treatment) which allowed for early interventions and care delivery (Fleming, 2000). An Alabama program focused on child passenger safety utilized an integrated care approach which included education, legislation, and training to implement safety protocols for children and realized a 75:1

ROI for every dollar spent (King, 2007). This is an example of drawing from a diverse sector of models to implement an effective model.

The ROI tends to grow as the program continues to run. For example, an Ohio program aimed at low-birth-weight children saw a first-year ROI of 3.36:1. Over the long term, the return grew to 5.59:1. Clearly, integrated care be it in education, safety, health, or mental health is a powerful tool for the profitability of healthcare institutions.

Who is Caring for Staff?

Healthcare has an elephant in the room. You cannot discuss the ethics or business of healthcare without addressing burnout, which is the negative effect an employee experiences as a result of the disparity between job demands and their personal resources.

The term "burnout" was coined in the 1970s when clinical psychologist Herbert Freudenberger saw first-hand the long-term effects of occupational stress in a free clinic in New York City. He noted that clinic staff was exhausted from "excessive demands on energy, strength, and resources." Moreover, Freudenberger observed that burnout was most prevalent in professions that required personal involvement and empathy (Reith, 2018).

Burned-out physicians claim that the source of their occupational stress is completing bureaucratic tasks, such as documentation and paperwork required by private insurance companies, Medicare, and Medicaid. Burnout was also attributed to spending too many hours at work, and the computerization of the medical field (Reith, 2018). Other contributors to burnout include high workloads, insufficient support, and poorly defined roles (Devilly, 2009).

A decade after burnout was named, social psychologist Christina Maslach developed the Maslach Burnout Inventory (MBI) model and identified the three dimensions of burnout: (1) Emotional exhaustion; (2) depersonalization (i.e., feeling disconnected from your body and like you are observing yourself from a different perspective); and (3) a diminished sense of personal accomplishment.

Burnout results in the perfect storm of behavioral health and substance abuse issues. The psychological outcomes of burnout manifest in the form of anxiety, depression, fatigue, and lack of motivation (Awa, Plaumann, & Walter, 2010). These psychological outcomes increase the odds of physician substance abuse and alcohol dependency. Even more disturbing is the statistic that physicians "are at an increased risk of suicide (28–40 per 100,000) compared to the general population (12.3 per 100,000)" (Patel, 2018).

The feeling of apathy and hopelessness, rapid exhaustion, disillusionment, melancholy, and forgetfulness are just a few key indicators. Signs and symptoms of vicarious traumatization are a risk factor for integrated healthcare systems as well and should be included in the readiness assessment. Therefore, over-identification with clients, feelings of great vulnerability and alienation, social withdrawal and disconnection from loved ones, and general despair or loss of confidence in the world are just a few to consider (Pearlman & Saakvitne, 1995).

There is a correlation between job burnout and the increased risk of developing secondary traumatic stress (STS) among human service professionals. STS encompasses symptoms including intrusion of memories or bodily experiences which interfere with your daily life, re-experiencing the traumatic experience both physically and psychologically, and avoidance of place, people, or experiences which reminds one of the traumatic event that results from indirect exposure to trauma, which is especially common in human service professionals (e.g., social workers, military health providers, and general trauma therapists) (Shoji, 2015). A study of Australian psychologists, psychotherapists, and clinical social workers found that burnout resulting from work-related stressors was a stronger predictor of therapist distress—in the form of depression, anxiety, and stress—than exposure to traumatic material (Devilly, 2009).

Burnout also leads to high turnover and absenteeism. Researchers have cited employee retention as a major issue in their organizations. One study found that nearly 50% of surveyed substance abuse treatment center direct service workers wanted to quit. High employee turnover is detrimental to both patients and organizations. Turnover jeopardizes patient continuity of care and financially burdens organizations with hiring and training new employees (Paris, 2010). The cost of losing an employee to burnout or job dissatisfaction can range from 90% to 200% of that employee's annual salary (Wallach, 2012). At a broader level, high employee turnover is an issue that threatens entire systems of healthcare, especially the mental health and substance use disorder (SUD) field (Hoge, 2013).

Healthcare practitioner burnout trickles down and severely impacts patient care. According to research, there is a correlation between medical errors committed by a surgeon during operation and the level of burnout the surgeon was experiencing. Moreover, nurses who were experiencing burnout had higher rates of patient mortality and hospital-transmitted infections (Reith, 2018). Researchers (Garman, 2002) surveyed staff and clients of 48 behavioral health programs in the midwestern United States and found that there was a correlation between staff burnout and patient satisfaction.

The symptoms of burnout are commonly found in the helping professions such as physicians, nurses, social workers, and teachers (Awa, Plaumann, & Walter, 2010). Burnout is insidious and common among healthcare practitioners. In the United States, 51% of physicians and 43% of nurses feel the effects of burnout (Reith, 2018). For physicians, the prevalence of burnout is significantly higher in outpatient facilities than in inpatient facilities (Patel, 2018).

Physicians are beginning to feel the effects of burnout early in their careers, oftentimes during their residency training (Patel, 2018). In fact, the Accreditation Council for Graduate Medical Education (ACGME) initiative Back to Bedside has funded thirty projects focused on patient-physician engagement and physician wellness (Accreditation Council for Graduate Medical Education, 2021). Medical schools are being proactive by educating their students about burnout. Vanderbilt University, for example, has created a wellness program that requires students to keep each other accountable. Students are given objectives throughout their medical training focused on surviving versus thriving while understanding the difference, motivated abilities which connect one's natural talents, conflict resolution while still working as a team member, and integration and choices which requires putting these objectives into practice. This forum is where faculty model self-care, contemplate oneself which will be reflected in one's physician role, and explore the giving relationship in medicine (Reith, 2018).

The impact on healthcare providers cannot be underestimated when collaboration is practiced. The ACGME's (Accreditation Council for Graduate Medical Education, 2021) recent focus on well-being for healthcare providers makes it clear that a physician's professional identity must fundamentally transform. Their knowledge, attitude, and behavior must align with patients, colleagues, and society as a whole.

Demonstration of this new professional conduct includes having accountability, humanism, and cultural proficiency. It also includes maintaining emotional, physical, and mental health within the context of continual personal and professional growth. Physicians need to take better care of themselves, in other words, and they need to consider self-care a basic part of their jobs.

But how can one person model all these traits? Becoming a physician already requires someone to have a high level of intellect and professional commitment. This new model then requires the physician to embrace curiosity, problem-solving, intellectual rigor, and awareness of the roles and values of all healthcare team members. On top of everything, they must be focused on their own wellness.

But with integrated care, the standard is actually relaxed. The PCP no longer has to be an expert in mental health. Now, there is a BHP right down the hall who is available to do quick assessments. The PCP no longer has to be an expert in everything. In this model, providers feel like part of a team. That improves enthusiasm for adoption.

Despite this element of relaxation, integrated care indeed poses high standards for providers to embody. But it results in better care for patients, fewer errors, and a lower risk of leaving the profession. The self-care strategies are enhanced by the integrated care model, which improves learning, reinforces coping, and makes working environments more attractive. In this way, integrated care directly reduces burnout.

Also, if professionals are working on health teams, they are more likely to have earlier identification and intervention of their distress, depression, and suicidal ideations or risk factors. In 2017, the ACGME committed the subsequent two years to working groups focused on leadership engagement, breaking the culture of silence, organizational best practices, workload and workflow process analysis, and other initiatives to address burnout (Accreditation Council for Graduate Medical Education, 2021). And a resounding message of "Let's Work Together" has been broadcast by a call to collect and share data, share joint research, share insights, share tools and resources, and create a better world for practicing within the healthcare theater (Brigham, 2019).

Another way that integrated care helps employees is by fostering job satisfaction. Increased engagement by employees leads to greater team cohesion. When each member knows their role is valued, they have a greater sense of fulfillment in their work. This will not only bring about better job performance but also cut down on attrition. Engaged and satisfied professionals are less likely to leave their positions and look for other work, thereby reducing the time and expense needed for recruiting and training new staff members.

More SUD healthcare workers are needed today than ever as the death rate for overdose and suicide escalates annually. The need for a more diverse workforce is needed as addiction has no race, gender, ethnic, or cultural boundaries. Access to care has increased with the Affordable Care Act of 2014, yet less than 10% of those suffering are diagnosed or attended to in the SUD or behavioral health sector of healthcare because of a lack of formal training on assessment.

Integrated care makes sense on many levels. Its ability to provide better care, lower cost, and make health services available to more people means that it is preferable from an ethical standpoint. From a business point of view, it allows us to do what we do for more people at considerable savings and makes good sense from a marketing and patient experience perspective.

Lower costs mean higher profitability and healthier higher human capital. In addition, satisfied patients—just like satisfied customers for any business—are more likely to recommend the health provider to others. The increased integration within the community also raises the center's profile. Finally, engaged employees report higher job satisfaction, which increases their productivity and lowers turnover costs.

No matter how you measure it, integrated care is a good idea.

References

Accreditation Council for Graduate Medical Education. (2021). *Back to bedside*. Retrieved from Accreditation Council for Graduate Medical Education: https://www.acgme.org/Residents-and-Fellows/Back-to-Bedside

Accreditation Council for Graduate Medical Education. (2021). www.acgme.org. Retrieved from Accreditation Council for Graduate Medical Education: https://www.acgme.org/

Awa, W. L., Plaumann, M., & Walter, U. (2009). Burnout prevention: A review of intervention programs. *Patient Education and Counseling*, 78(2), 184–190.

Brigham, T. (2019). Physician well-being initiative. *Federation physician health annual meeting*.

Cohen, D. C. (2015). *A guidebook of professional practices for behavioral health and primary care integration: Observations From exemplary sites*. Rockville, MD: Agency for Healthcare Research and Quality.

COPA Health. (2020). *About*. Retrieved from https://copahealth.org/about/

Devilly, G. W. (2009). Vicarious trauma, secondary traumatic stress or simply burnout? Effect of trauma therapy on mental health professionals. *Australian and New Zealand Journal of Psychiatry*, 43(4), 373–385.

Fleming, M. F. (2000). Benefit-cost analysis of brief physician advice with problem drinkers in primary care settings. *Medical Care*, 38(1), 7–18.

Garman, A. N. (2002). Staff burnout and patient satisfaction: Evidence of relationships at the care unit level. *Journal of Occupational Health Psychology*, 7(3), 235–241.

Hoge, M. A. (2013). Mental health and addiction workforce development: Federal leadership is needed to address the growing crisis. *Health Affairs (Project Hope)*, 32(11), 2005–2012.

King, W. D.-F. (2007). The impact of education, legislation and service on Alabama child passenger safety. *Journal of Trauma and Acute Care Surgery*, 63(3), 525–528.

Mackenzie, Maureen L. Ph.D. & Wallach, Darren F. MBA (2012). The Boss-Employee Relationship: Influence on Job Retention. *Faculty Works: Business*, 11. https://digitalcommons.molloy.edu/bus_fac/11.

Paris, M. & Hoge, M. A. (2010). Burnout in the mental health workforce: A review. *Journal of Behavioral Health Services & Research*, 37(4), 519–528.

Patel, R. S. (2018). Factors related to physician burnout and its consequences: A review. *Behavioral Sciences*, 8(11), 98.

Pearlman, L., & Saakvitne, K. W. (1995). *Trauma and the therapist: Countertransference and vicarious traumatization in psychotherapy with incest survivors* (1st ed.). New York: Norton.

Reith, T. P. (2018). Burnout in United States healthcare professionals: A narrative review. *Cureus*, 10(12).

Shoji, K. L. (2015). What comes first, job burnout or secondary traumatic stress? Findings from two longitudinal studies from the US and Poland. *PLOS One*, 10(8), e0136730–e0136730

6 Whole Person Care

From its beginnings in the 1950s as Chit Chat Farms, today's Caron Treatment Centers were always providing multidisciplinary care. Its earliest iteration was simply a family's home, with the doors open to people struggling with alcohol abuse. But even then, it was not just a place to get sober. It was also a place for the family to access support to help repair their own trauma. That whole-person, systemic approach stemmed from the founder's own struggle with addiction.

In its modern form, Caron is investing heavily in the integration of medical services into its treatment programs. The company opened a 50,000-square-foot medical center in 2017. This center allows Caron to treat patients who struggle with significant medical comorbidities, alongside substance use and psychological disorders.

Bradley Sorte was committed to Caron's vision from the beginning of his career. His first job in psychology was as an overnight behavioral health tech at a treatment center that then promoted him to a group therapist case manager. In that position, he learned all about working with the substance use disorder (SUD) population, on both an individual and group basis. When he went back to school for a graduate degree, he always knew he wanted to end up with Caron—in large part because of the family treatment program.

"If we can really help change the social context that people with substance use disorder come from, we can set them up for a much better chance of success down the road—because whatever that system they came from will be a more healthy-functioning system, [with] better boundaries and more transparent communication," said Sorte. "And if anyone in that family has any of their own underlying issues, hopefully they can be identified and addressed, so that when a person who's the identified patient finishes treatment, the whole family dynamic would be healthier."

Programs to support the family are especially important for medical health homes that serve certain populations. Practices that serve children, for example, need to provide educational support that enables mothers, fathers, or other caregivers to address their children's health needs. These

DOI: 10.4324/9781003128571-6

services can help families find community services that help them cope with challenges. The presence of a BHP allows the family to receive counseling to help them deal with the emotional stress of a sick child.

Family support is absolutely critical in the context of substance abuse treatment centers. Addiction is a disease that affects the entire family, not just the person using alcohol and/or other drugs. Family programs in this setting often address two aspects. The first is the healing of the family members. They have experienced the pain caused by a loved one's addiction and have dealt with the disruption and stress it causes in their lives. They need a chance to heal from this trauma and restore their relationship with the person in recovery. The second includes behaviors by family members that may have contributed to or enabled the addiction. Modifying such patterns is vital to preventing relapse.

In the early stages of addiction treatment, those involved brought lived experience and passion. That lived experience continues to be critical, and yet today's crisis has no boundaries and requires all of healthcare's attention. It requires not just detox support—from both doctors and BHPs—and family treatment, but much broader interdisciplinary involvement.

One set of individual and interpersonal practices that contribute to whole care revolve around the structure and timing of care delivery. It is generally appreciated but cannot be repeated often enough: Earlier diagnosis of behavioral issues, particularly SUDs, generally leads to better treatment outcomes. Plus, it averts the personal tragedies that can result from the longevity of use. Richard Caron, who co-founded Caron Treatment Centers with his wife Catherine, was an alcoholic himself. And the longevity of his illness was brutal. He had multiple convictions for drunk driving, was fired from the family business, went through inpatient treatment, and put Catherine through six years of unknowable stress before he took his last drink.

When discussing intervention in public health, we often speak of primary, secondary, and tertiary prevention (L'Abate, 2007). For SUDs, tertiary treatment involves inpatient detox and rehabilitation. This late-stage, acute treatment is mainly the domain of behavioral health/addiction specialists due to biopsychosocial deterioration.

The fact that SUDs in traditional healthcare are most often treated only after the disease state has taken hold is a tragedy. This late-stage treatment often takes the forms of detoxification and residential treatment. These tertiary interventions are extremely expensive and usually come only after the illness has wreaked havoc on the individual's health, family, career, and community.

In the integrated care implementations I have led, my goal has always been on transferring substance use treatments to an early stage in the disorder's development. These treatments could occur at an early sign of a problem (e.g., therapy or 12-step group participation suggested by a care coordinator) or even as a preventive measure [e.g., a screening or risk assessment performed by a primary care provider (PCP)].

Integrated care can move substance use interventions upstream to secondary interventions and—whenever possible—to the stage of primary interventions. The secondary intervention involves screening after problematic onset but before serious complications develop. This allows treating the misuse of substances in the early stages to prevent a full-blown disorder from developing. This could entail a primary care physician, cardiologist, OB/GYN, pediatrician, or other specialist screening for problems in order to detect them as early as possible.

Even better is primary intervention, which requires enhanced professional education, national guidelines and standards for assessment and treatment, identifying at-risk patients (e.g., utilization of the Adverse Childhood Effects (ACE) instrument), patient education, and risk assessment to head off problems before they start (Kolodny, 2015).

Addiction is by no means the first crisis encountered by the healthcare profession, and we can learn from our response to previous diseases and epidemics. One example of moving the response from tertiary to primary intervention is found in the case of smallpox, a disease that had been around for thousands of years. To this day, the treatment of smallpox once it has developed is quite limited, with a focus on isolating the patient and the treatment of skin wounds. No drug has been shown to be effective in the treatment of a patient once infected.

Despite this, smallpox is considered to have been eradicated by the 1970s due to major efforts aimed at primary intervention. Although the use of inoculation against smallpox dates to as early as the eighth century, true vaccination was not developed until the 1800s. Its widespread use during the following century eradicated the disease. Because of primary intervention against smallpox, tertiary care is rarely needed in modern medicine. The invention and use of the polio vaccine illustrate the same principle, although polio has not yet been fully eradicated.

The HIV/AIDS epidemic of the 1980s and 1990s provides an example of how integrated care can help slow the spread of disease. While medical treatments for HIV have continued to improve and signs are promising that a vaccine for the disease may soon be available, the epidemic has been best addressed by educational campaigns carried out by both medical and behavioral health professionals.

In the US, the number of deaths rose dramatically during the 1980s, reaching a peak of 41,699 deaths from AIDS in 1995. As primary intervention became widespread, the numbers began to decrease just as quickly. Educating people at risk about behaviors that help spread the disease (e.g., unprotected sex and the use of infected needles) has had a profound effect. The same results have been seen worldwide, with AIDS-related deaths declining by 48% since their apex in 2005 (United Nations Programme on HIV/AIDS, 2017). New cases of HIV infection are also in decline, with the number of cases in the US dropping 18% from 2008 to 2014 (Minority HIV/AIDS Fund, 2021). The intervention has been a cooperative effort by both the medical and behavioral health fields.

Lessons learned from smallpox and AIDS could improve the treatment of a wide variety of disorders and illnesses. Transferring care upstream to primary and secondary interventions can improve outcomes in COVID-19, for example.

But because addiction is such an ideal illustration (and because it is my area of expertise), let us focus on that. The rest of this chapter paints a picture of what it looks like when integrated care is fully implemented in the context of addiction treatment.

Primary and Secondary Interventions

PCPs are often the first line of defense against addiction. Educating people on the risks of addiction is a necessary part of prevention (i.e., primary intervention), and those PCPs who typically see their patients on a regular basis are in the best position to provide information and reinforcement of knowledge about addiction. AHRQ's guidebook for integrated care says that patients should always be encouraged to take advantage of wellness programs when addressing all health and mental health needs provided by the clinic.

PCPs also have the best chance of detecting the early signs of addiction—and providing secondary intervention. Aside from prevention, early detection is one of the most successful tools in the fight against the addiction crisis.

PCPs who are educated about and are attentive to indicators of a SUD can refer patients to treatment providers before the addiction becomes more severe. SBIRT is an effective approach to combatting addiction model can be applied across numerous healthcare settings and actually serves as a brief treatment intervention by educating individuals by just asking questions relevant to SUD. SBIRT has been integrated into some WHO initiatives and is standard education in medical schools.

Behavioral health's role in addiction treatment is fairly well defined, given that substance use treatment has generally been considered to be the purview of mental health providers. But the field of behavioral health needs to move toward integrated care, breaking down the barriers to communication with those in the medical field.

The psychiatrist has a place on both the medical and clinical teams. On the medical side, their responsibilities include ruling out medical issues before a behavioral health diagnosis is issued. In my work as a sex therapist, I had to integrate the patient's medical history with their relational and sexual history, as well as any co-occurring disorders. I often had to rule out physiological issues which play a prominent role in these disorders. For this task, the more communication with the medical staff and psychiatrist, the better. I never wanted to start going down the path of psychological treatment or couples therapy if the disorder stemmed from a physical disease state. This oversight would not reflect best practices, evidence-based care, or professional decision-making.

On the clinical team, the psychiatrist's job is to monitor the patient's mental health problems from a medical standpoint, identify and order consultations, integrate medical knowledge into the care, and adjust any medications they are being given. They work in collaboration with the psychologists and treatment team to continually assess the patient's progress and determine the best course of treatment. This process requires a significant amount of communication and agility, as data-informed decisions with thoughtful coordination are the rule. Treatment is not always a straight line. Providers can no longer afford to be rigid. Flux is the rule rather than the exception, and providers have to stay open to many determinants that are influencing a patient's disorder—as well as the many responses that may help resolve it. Having a multidisciplinary team is key to maintaining that openness and agility.

Addiction treatment professionals have a role in serving as consultants to those in medicine, helping them to recognize the signs of addiction. They must also be available for referrals, which means developing relationships with medical professionals. These cooperative relationships are essential to addressing the current addiction crisis via primary and secondary interventions.

Another incredibly important aspect of moving interventions upstream is the promotion of health. This goes beyond the treatment of particular acute symptoms to programs that encourage healthier lifestyles, such as nutrition counseling, 12-step meetings, exercise programs, and smoking cessation programs. Also included in this area is the management of chronic conditions such as diabetes, hypertension, asthma, and arthritis.

One component of health promotion—and one that is often overlooked—is working with patients to remove possible barriers to treatment or make treatment accessible. Issues such as transportation, childcare, geographic locations, and insurance can interfere with patients' ability to keep appointments. This is particularly true in behavioral health settings but will increasingly be the case in primary care as integration proceeds. As a complete health home, it is important for all staff within the organization to work with patients to overcome these barriers and not just rely on the traditional models of clinical social workers or case managers to be responsible.

Tertiary Interventions

Detox is generally the first stage of any recovery program. Although withdrawal from some substances carries lower risks than others, medically monitored detox is the safest approach. For some substances, it is an absolute necessity due to life-threatening symptoms such as suicidal thoughts, hallucinations, and seizures. Just consider the American Society of Addiction Medicine (ASAM) withdrawal management criteria when determining whether ambulatory, residential, or inpatient monitoring is warranted. An individual's impairment of liver functioning, risk of seizures or other comorbid conditions that can be exacerbated by hyperarousal, or pregnancy can all increase the severity and risk during withdrawal. The interaction of substances with psychiatric medications can increase the potential of disorganization during withdrawal. Another factor to consider is whether the individual is 'ready for change' as some level of motivation is required for withdrawal compliance to be effective. Finally, is the individual still at risk for continued use of the substance, and do they have adequate support systems in place to assist with care during this vulnerable period? All of these variables must be taken into consideration as they impact both engagement of the individual and the care provider's comfort and recommendations.

A medical detox not only improves patient safety but can also reduce the discomfort associated with withdrawal. Although many people go through detox before being admitted to a recovery center, some addiction treatment facilities have their own on-site detox units. During the medical management of detox and withdrawal, therapists begin formulating a recovery plan while offering alternatives for cravings (e.g., education, 12-step orientation and etiquette, cognitive-behavioral recovery skills, and developing relapse prevention skills). The value of having medical attention during this phase also stems from the potential that undiagnosed or ignored medical conditions can be properly assessed and treated simultaneously, resulting in enhanced remission.

The medical education component of treatment may consist of what to expect when withdrawing, coping strategies, medication education, and treatment planning. It may include education on post-acute withdrawal syndrome (PAWS), in which withdrawal symptoms can last for as much as a year. It may include education on medical distress tolerance, which is the complications, discomfort, long-term commitment required, and need to manage stressors in one's life without the aid of the substance.

The individualized plan includes goals and objectives. The plan should be inclusive of patient input. It is a working, dynamic document updated frequently with progress, barriers, completion of goals, and new objectives.

Modern addiction treatment requires two teams of specialists to care for the whole person: A medical team and a clinical team. This delineation is not as dichotomous as it sounds. Initially, the medical team is primarily responsible for the physical well-being of the patients as they are the primary providers during the detoxification process, which constitutes the first phase of treatment. They continue to help restore the patient to safety and health in the post-detox period while being responsible for any medically assisted treatment. Meanwhile, the clinical team begins stabilization, orientation, and assessment during the detox period with supportive brief therapy. This counseling offers a bridge once the patient has finished detox. The two teams may each have their own treatment goals but will coordinate and prioritize the order of care while being aware of both treatment plans. Hence, integrated care is in its most simplistic definition.

The roles and responsibilities of each member of the medical and clinical teams intersect, which is why coordination within and between the teams is paramount.

The medical field plays a major role in addiction treatment through its involvement in the withdrawal management stage of care under the integrated care model. The medical team is led by a physician and/or physician extenders (e.g., nurse practitioner or physician assistant) specializing in some aspect of addiction medicine. These medical providers are responsible for the initial examination of the patient. During this assessment, they will decide which medical specialists, of which there are 120 (Association of American Medical Colleges, 2021), need to be brought in to treat the patient. Different substances affect the body in so many different ways, and their effects can vary based on the longevity of use, genetic factors of the individual, environmental conditions, and intensity of the substance use.

The physician and/or medical providers will tailor a medically based program to fit the patient's needs and determine the best course of treatment, which is usually delivered and monitored by nursing staff. The physician and extenders, with assistance from nursing staff, are responsible for coordinating care between the specialists, interpreting testing and laboratory results, following the progress of the patient while making medication adjustments, envisioning long-term care recommendations, and fostering communication between everyone involved.

By no means is this an exhaustive description of the responsibilities by the physician or medical extenders. The electronic health record (EHR) documentation requirements, insurance certifications, disability determination, and Family and Medical Leave Act (FMLA) assistance are just a few examples of the necessary tasks that require a physician.

A psychiatrist is an integral member of the medical team as well, meeting with the patient after acute withdrawal to diagnose any co-occurring mental health problems that may complicate the treatment of the SUD. Among these are depression, anxiety disorders, OCD, eating disorders, PTSD, and unprocessed past trauma, including abuse and sexual assault. These will need to be addressed alongside the addiction because they often serve as one of the contributing factors to addiction. The psychiatrist is responsible for managing any prescriptions used to treat these disorders and can also monitor instances of polypharmacy. These medications can often interact in ways that are detrimental to the patient's health because of limited knowledge on drug interactions within the literature.

Medication management is crucial to integrated care. Currently, the majority of drugs prescribed for behavioral health problems are prescribed by PCPs, usually in collaboration with a psychiatric consultant. This includes not only the initial prescription but also their ongoing use.

Within an integrated care setting that includes a psychiatrist, this process can be improved by the psychiatrist handling the prescriptions. But even when a psychiatrist is not a part of the team, the collaboration between the PCP and a psychiatric consultant can be improved through the use of the onsite non-physician BHP. Although these clinicians cannot prescribe medications, they are in a position to facilitate communication between PCPs and psychiatric consultants and help PCPs identify and understand the underlying psychological condition. The presence of the BHP can also discourage the practice of individuals who use pharmacotherapy without participating in mental health therapy.

The multidisciplinary team should also include a physician specializing in pain recovery. As discussed in the context of the history of addiction, one of the factors driving the current opioid crisis is the rise in the prescribing of opioid painkillers (Centers for Disease Control and Prevention, 2018). Some of this increase is due to doctors being increasingly willing to prescribe opioids for chronic pain. Many of the people who are currently using heroin began by using a legal prescription opioid under medical supervision. When such a patient enters treatment for addiction, it is often the case that chronic pain is still present. Without the painkillers, chronic pain can once again become intolerable.

Pain recovery specialists are able to help people control their chronic pain through non-pharmaceutical means or through the use of non-addictive analgesics and alternative physical treatments. A physiatrist (a doctor specializing in physical medicine and rehabilitation) and physical therapist may assist with removing the pain and gaining control, removing one of the major impetuses for taking opioids.

Because of the internal physical damage that can be caused by the misuse of drugs and alcohol, an internist should be part of the medical team. Alcohol use, for instance, is associated with several types of cancer, including esophageal, lip, oral cavity, pharynx, and larynx. Other diseases connected to alcohol are acute and chronic pancreatitis, cirrhosis, chronic hepatitis, pulmonary tuberculosis, hypertension, cerebrovascular disease, and diabetes (Kington, 2002). Because the risk of these problems goes up with increased alcohol usage, alcoholics often need the specialty care of an internist.

Alcohol and most illicit drugs can also cause cardiovascular problems (National Institute on Drug Abuse, 2020). Heart attacks, irregular heartbeat, coronary heart disease, and tachycardia can all be triggered by substance use. Those who abuse alcohol are particularly vulnerable to heart disease. Multidisciplinary teams should include a cardiologist trained in addiction medicine who can address these problems in patients.

Other internal problems can be caused as well. For example, opioids can cause a condition known as opioid-induced bowel dysfunction. This condition includes a number of gastrointestinal symptoms such as constipation, anorexia, nausea, vomiting, delayed digestion, and abdominal pain—all of which need to be addressed by an internist (Leppert, 2012).

Immunology is another specialization that should be part of the multidisciplinary team. Research has shown that alcohol abuse can create immunodeficiency that allows the development of pneumonia, tuberculosis, hepatitis, and other conditions (National Institute on Alcohol Abuse and Alcoholism, 2000). In fact, several studies have suggested that liver disease in alcoholics may in part be caused by an alcohol-triggered autoimmune response. Opioids and cocaine can also wreak havoc on the immune system (Halpern, 2003). Immunology specialists are necessary to help addicts return to full health.

Because of the importance of gender-specific treatment, the medical team should also include a gynecologist and urologist. The majority of women who suffer from addictions have experienced trauma, often in the form of sexual assault. Other types of physical assaults can have effects on reproductive health. A significant number of substance use patients—both women and men—have engaged in risky behavior that has increased the likelihood of sexually transmitted disease. All these conditions in women are best addressed by a gynecologist or urologist.

These examples are in no way intended to be an exhausted list of specialty medical care providers required to provide whole health to patients suffering from addiction, but simply highlight the complexity required to address the more common ailments.

The medical team is rounded out by physician assistants and nurses, including nurse practitioners and psychiatric nurse practitioners. These clinicians are integral extenders delivering key core competencies. The nursing challenges involved in treating people with SUDs are many. They should have a background in addiction treatment to be able to address these complex disorders adequately and embrace a holistic approach to patient care. Nurses are the backbone of the treatment team as they fluidly monitor and intervene on patients throughout the bio-psycho-social-spiritual transformation.

While recruiting medical providers to provide this integrated care may seem daunting, today's medical education has shifted to include etiology and public health impact of addiction, evaluation for substance use and SUDs, pharmacological treatment of SUDs, psychosocial treatment of all ailments, and overdose prevention training (Tetrault, 2017).

On the clinical side, the majority of care is done by those with master's degrees. These include counselors with addiction training, clinical social workers, mental health counselors, and marriage and family counselors. Any of these different clinicians can serve as the primary therapist/care provider during treatment. In that role, they are responsible for coordinating the treatment of their patients by the various specialists and for ensuring that communication is taking place between the appropriate treatment providers.

Case managers have the responsibility of overseeing the patient's case, making sure that all aspects of treatment are working together and all the patient's needs both internally and externally are being addressed. While the primary counselor has the ultimate responsibility for this coordination, the case managers can help provide an overall view of the patient's use of services. They focus not only on addiction treatment but also on the patient's interaction with other aspects of the treatment center, such as career services, disability needs, FMLA, medication procurement, financial management, and insurance. They are also a good source for data collection as engagement is usually high with these individuals.

After Detox

The clinical team has primary responsibility for patients after they leave detox, though the medical team is still very much involved in this phase of treatment. However, having clinical programming that matches the needs of patients during this phase encourages engagement and flow towards goals. Not only qualified clinical staff but also physical therapy staff are necessary to assist with both physical and mental atrophy and can aid in the transition from PAWS. For example, having a visit to the bedside by a physical therapist or a walk around the facility improves motivation and engagement.

The clinical team at this point continues to include members with various levels of training, including doctoral-level practitioners (e.g., psychologists, psychiatrists, mental health counselors, and social workers), master's-level clinicians (e.g., social workers, addiction counselors, marriage and family therapists, and spiritual counselors), and bachelor's-level personnel (e.g., certified addiction counselors, case managers, aftercare specialists, recovery coaches, and interventionists).

On a clinical team, psychologists (PhD) and psychiatrists (MD) have distinct but complementary roles. The psychologists on the team specialize in behavioral health approaches to addiction. They are major contributors to the primary diagnosis. They meet with the client after they has detoxed. These meetings are usually for testing and assessment. The psychologists' diagnosis is then used to formulate a treatment plan to address the patient's addiction and any co-occurring disorders from a behavioral health standpoint. The treatment plan is coordinated with the master's-level clinicians and nursing staff, who have been conducting their own assessments and diagnosis. This combined treatment plan allows for a unified assessment focusing on the history of substance use, developmental experiences and formulations, life stressors, coping capacity, personality structure, emotion tolerance, affect regulation, primary/secondary defense mechanisms, strengths, spirituality, family history, and social support systems. The individual's voice and perception of the problem must be considered. These self-directed needs and perception of their hierarchy of needs are fully considered and integrated into the plan. The psychologists continue to monitor the patient through the clinical phase, updating the assessment and adjusting the treatment plan as needed.

During this longer stage of the tertiary intervention, counselors work with patients one-on-one and in group settings. They help patients through the 12 Steps, Cognitive Behavioral Therapy, Motivational Interviewing, Trauma-Informed Care, Relapse Prevention, Contingency Management, and other modes of behavioral counseling. In addition to discussions meant to help patients address the roots of their addiction, counselors also provide skill training. Topics covered may include step work, drug and alcohol refusal skills training, problem-solving, identifying cognitive distortions, coping strategies, vocational skills, recovery etiquette, personality assessment, trauma resolution, and social skills training.

Lapse behavior is a rich topic to cover in these sessions. Patients should identify high-risk situations and discuss how to avoid them, along with other relapse prevention and remission optimization strategies.

Licensed clinical social workers (LCSWs) are social workers who are trained in assessment while addressing mental, physical, and emotional health issues. Those at an addiction treatment facility will provide all of the above interventions and should have specialized training in SUDs with co-occurring disorders. Often, they will provide similar types of psychotherapy that are similar to those provided by a counselor, despite different training. The two roles have similar responsibilities that are a blend of case management, treatment planning, aftercare coordination, individual therapy, family therapy, and group facilitation. Because they often provide counseling to family groups, they also overlap to a certain extent with the next group.

Marriage and family counselors are an important part of the clinical team because addiction is a disease that affects the entire family and multiple systems. In recent decades, the role of family members in enabling substance use has been increasingly recognized and discouraged. In order for someone with a SUD to maintain recovery, relationships within the family must be healed and destructive behaviors on the part of the rest of the family must be addressed.

But the role of marriage and family counselors is not limited to helping the individual identified patient. Family members have also been hurt by their loved one's actions. They need to heal just as much as the person with the SUD.

The people in other impacted systems should also be given the opportunity to have open, honest, and direct conversations with the individual. For example, in my extensive experience working with healthcare providers on their own behavioral health issues, I found that one of the important elements of their recovery was often addressing the workplace team. Personality characteristics and traits are usually demonstrated within the context of the work system very similar to family dynamics. Individuals often take on roles in the workplace similar to their family of origin which need to be openly discussed with other healthcare team members to better understand what the environment was like before the individual was removed and while they were absent from the work environment.

So, prior to discharge from treatment, I would visit their workplace with them. We would take a day or two of accountability sessions with stakeholders there. These meetings would give all stakeholders the opportunity to deal with the patient's behavior and their response to them. What was it like to work with them before they came to treatment? What has it been like without them in the workplace? What are the fears or concerns about this person re-entering into this system?

And vocational settings are not the only impacted systems. Extended support networks, intimate relationships, communal and spiritual systems, judicial, legal, and correctional systems are just a few who can benefit from individual accountability sessions.

Expressive therapists play a crucial role on the team, as assessment, treatment, and monitoring are beyond talk therapy. These clinicians are usually master's prepared and may specialize in movement, art, or music therapy. Addiction has overwhelmed the sensory systems, and rewards have provided reinforcements that often cannot be articulated verbally. Therefore, a mix of expressive therapies must be accessed in order to heal areas of the brain, body, and spirit.

These sensory-filled experiences allow a reconfiguration of life's narrative and metaphors (e.g., being a beginner, learning something with fresh eyes, observing things forgotten by the power of addiction, recognizing the incompleteness in the healing journey, overcoming adversity, protracted commitment, healing turmoil, and relying on others). These are just some of the possible needs that can be integrated with expressive techniques.

Finally, there is the unique group of health and wellness staff who empower the entire system of healing for the individual. These are professionally trained staff who have identified the integrated nature of their work and who are fitness trainers, exercise physiologists, professional ropes course facilitators, physical therapists, massage therapists, nutritionists, and yoga instructors.

The opportunity to be led by experts in fitness to a healthy lifestyle should really be at the top of this list. SUDs damage every cell in one's body. They cause neuro-lethargy and musculature atrophy. Being shown proper exercise techniques with a written plan is a corrective experience for most. Listening to the description of the exercise and nutritional myths offers an opportunity for teachable moments. Clarifying human anatomy and physiology facts while developing a healthy eating plan with cooking demonstrations is the perfect recipe for reversing the physiological impacts of addiction. The commitment to understanding eating healthy versus dieting is paramount to recovery from SUDs.

Adding fitness facilities is appropriate in residential care facilities—not just those for addiction treatment but also for long-term treatment of cognitive impairment. Physical activity improves mood, decreases cravings, and increases cognitive functions. It has been shown to be helpful in the treatment of substance abuse (Williams, 2004). Having fitness centers, swimming pools, yoga rooms, and outdoor space for team sports in residential facilities for behavioral health is also in keeping with the integration of behavioral and somatic health and the promotion of overall wellness (Facility Guidelines Institute, 2018).

A number of other bachelor's-level/lived experience positions round out the long-term tertiary intervention treatment team. These include case managers, aftercare/discharge planners, and recovery coaches. These roles assist in the coordination of communication, prepare the patients to connect with services in the community after discharge, and serve as a resource for patients who need continued help in their recovery.

Aftercare or discharge planners help patients transition into their life after treatment. They work with the clients to develop a recovery plan that continues after they leave the facility. Part of this involves connecting them with resources in the community, such as 12-step meetings, sponsors, and sober-living facilities. Aftercare planners work within a recovery-oriented system of care (ROSC), which is a network of local recovery resources that are geared toward helping people maintain sobriety.

Recovery peers/coaches are another part of the clinical team. Much in the same way that life coaches help people achieve life goals and fitness staff help people achieve fitness goals, recovery coaches are available to help people remain in recovery. Often, recovery coaches are themselves in recovery, so they are able to use their own experiences to help others who are new to recovery. Some coaches work in the community, while others are associated with treatment centers. Those at treatment centers serve as a connection between former patients and the center.

When people in recovery need help to maintain sobriety, recovery coaches are available to help. The core competencies include:

- Recovery-oriented: Peer workers hold out hope to those they serve, partnering with them to envision and achieve a meaningful and purposeful life. Peer workers help those they serve to identify and build on strengths and empower them to choose for themselves, recognizing that there are multiple pathways to recovery
- Person-centered: Peer recovery support services are always directed by the person participating in services. Peer recovery support is

personalized to align with the specific hopes, goals, and preferences of the individual served and to respond to specific needs the individuals have identified to the peer worker
- Voluntary: Peer workers are partners or consultants to those they serve. They do not dictate the types of services provided or the elements of recovery plans that will guide their work with peers. Participation in peer recovery support services is always contingent on peer choice
- Relationship-focused: The relationship between the peer worker and the peer is the foundation on which peer recovery support services and support are provided. The relationship between the peer worker and peer is respectful, trusting, empathetic, collaborative, and mutual
- Trauma-informed: Peer recovery support utilizes a strength-based framework that emphasizes physical, psychological, and emotional safety and creates opportunities for survivors to rebuild a sense of control and empowerment

Conclusion

This concludes my painting of a picture of integrated care in the context of addiction treatment. Clearly, the components of integrated care include a diverse range of people, facilities, and services.

The leadership is key in setting the tone and commitment to integrated care and ensuring that staff with the required expertise is in place and works diligently to remove all barriers for care delivery. The staff work as a team, meeting regularly for discussions of patients and ways to improve the process and patient experiences. Patient tracking allows the practice to provide measurement-based care, while family support and transitional services address broader issues of patient health. These components work together to provide the best healing environment where providers and employees develop their fullest potential in the areas of effectiveness, community stewardship, self-motivation, and future leadership capacity (Chen, 2015). This improved quality of service promotes interpersonal acceptance, authenticity, and psychological flexibility in both changing patient behavior and employees' understanding of their self-identity. The power of identifying one's internal processes and impact on others offers an opportunity to revise one's narrative of themselves and their relationships. Ultimately, this leads to empowerment, insight, and awareness.

The focus of the chapter has been on the system's talent, who require nutrients in order to thrive as a 'community of caring.' The need for highly efficient, complementary team members ultimately yields the best results. As you can see, this specialized group of professionals must be competent and agile. They must possess excellent communication skills and embrace an egalitarian approach where all voices are respected.

The team members must be able to self-regulate in the face of a highly charged environment, as addiction cases have so many facets that need to be sorted and addressed simultaneously. The functioning of the team is usually mirrored by the client community, that is, a parallel process. Therefore, a routine pause and reflection by each member of the professional team and its leadership will only serve to enhance the work environment and patient milieu.

References

Association of American Medical Colleges. (2021). *Speciality profiles*. Retrieved from Association of American Medical Colleges: https://www.aamc.org/cim/explore-options/specialty-profiles

Centers for Disease Control and Prevention. (2018, August 31). *Annual surveillance report of drug-related risks and outcomes – United States*. Retrieved from https://www.cdc.gov/drugoverdose/pdf/pubs/2018-cdc-drug-surveillance-report.pdf

Chen, Z. Z. (2015). How does a servant leader fuel the service fire? A multilevel model of servant leadership, individual self-identity, group competition climate, and customer service performance. *Journal of Applied Psychology, 100*(2), 511–521.

Facility Guidelines Institute. (2018). *2018 edition*. Retrieved from https://fgiguidelines.org/guidelines/2018-fgi-guidelines/

Halpern, J. H. (2003). Diminished interleukin-6 response to proinflammatory challenge in men and women after intravenous cocaine administration. *Journal of Clinical Endocrinol Metabolism, 88*, 1188–1193.

Kington, R. A. (2002). Internal medicine and alcohol-Time to move forward. *Journal of General Internal Medicine, 17*(4), 400–401. doi: 10.1007/s11606-002-0048-z

Kolodny, A. C. (2015). The prescription opioid and heroin crisis: A public health approach to an epidemic of addiction. *Annual Review of Public Health, 36*(1), 559–574.

L'Abate, L. (2007). *Low-Cost Approaches to Promote Physical and Mental Health: Theory, Research and Practice (1. Aufl.)*. Springer-Verlag. https://doi.org/10.1007/0-387-36899-X

Leppert, W. (2012). The impact of opioid analgesics on the gastrointestinal tract function and the current management possibilities. *Contemporary Oncology, 16*, 125–131. doi: 10.5114/wo.2012.28792

Minority HIV/AIDS Fund. (2021, March 17). *Fast facts*. Retrieved from HIV.gov: https://www.hiv.gov/hiv-basics/overview/data-and-trends/statistics

National Institute on Alcohol Abuse and Alcoholism. (2000). Tenth special report to the U.S. Congress on alcohol and health (pp. 214–226). Washington DC: US Department of Health and Human Services. Retrieved from https://pubs.niaaa.nih.gov/publications/10report/chap04b.pdf

National Institute on Drug Abuse. (2020, June). *Health consequences of drug misuse: Cardiovascular effects*. Retrieved from National Institute on Drug Abuse: https://www.drugabuse.gov/publications/health-consequences-drug-misuse/cardiovascular-effects/

Tetrault, J. M. (2017). Partnering with psychiatry to close the education gap: An approach to the addiction epidemic. *Journal of General Internal Medicine, 32*, 1387. doi: 10.1007/s11606-017-4140-9

United Nations Programme on HIV/AIDS. (2017). *Fact sheet: Latest statistics on the status of the AIDS epidemic.* Retrieved from http://www.unaids.org/sites/default/files/media_asset/UNAIDS_FactSheet_en.pdf.

Williams, D. J. (2004). Physical activity as a helpful adjunct to substance abuse treatment. *Journal of Social Work Practice in the Addictions, 4*(3), 83–100.

7 Care Coordination & Insurance Companies

Behavioral health care coordination is another hallmark of integrated care that helps to move interventions upstream to an earlier stage of treatment. Under the integrated care model, an individual provider takes responsibility for overseeing all the care provided to an individual patient.

Within a primary care setting, this is usually done by a PCP, while in a behavioral health setting it is usually a professional therapist. In both cases, however, this role can also be performed by any designated team member who has the requisite skills, credentials, and appropriate licensure. Care coordinators can be embedded in practice as staff, or they can be external (i.e., a contractor).

The care coordinator is incredibly valuable. They are responsible for determining not only the services that a patient needs but also the order in which issues are addressed. They are the contractor on the renovation of your dream house. This ensures that each client receives appropriate care, while also providing them with a single point of contact for health questions.

So why do not all patients have a dedicated care manager already? Many of the barriers are tied to issues of payment and insurance. That is why, in addition to the fields of medicine and behavioral health, we must also consider collaboration with one other player: The insurance industry. Although insurance providers would not generally be considered part of the treatment team, coordination with them is a necessary part of assessment, treatment, and monitoring. Communication about the nature and severity of the problem allows them to make informed decisions about which treatments to cover.

There are three main strategies to overcome the payment issue: Take advantage of existing (but under-utilized) billing codes, advocate for patients to receive higher levels of care earlier in their treatment, and increase profitability—and pass the savings on via financial assistance. Throughout all of these strategies, it is important to collaborate with payers, including by providing information about integrated care. Educating insurance providers, state and local government, and other payers about the benefits this model offers to them increases the

DOI: 10.4324/9781003128571-7

likelihood that they will cover treatment, which makes the care available to a larger patient population. I recall conveying this value to executive leaders by encouraging them to require behavioral health care coordination as more data can be collected between visits and utilized to inform medical decision-making. This monitoring improves the comfort of providers as well instead of relying only on monthly or quarterly visits. The intermediary collection of data by checking in and providing a brief assessment improves engagement and averts the unexpected need for a higher level of care.

Substance use disorder (SUD) admissions increased by 18% and mental health admissions increased by 6% between 2013 and 2017. This accounted for the largest percentage increase in all specialties while the cost of care increased 39% for SUD treatment and 14% for mental health during this period (Centers for Disease Control and Prevention, 2020).

Again, I recently provided decision support to another executive at a major health insurance company. I illustrated the lack of one of the most valuable services and the lack of funding to it. And I showed that, if that billing code's utilization was just boosted by roughly 20% (e.g., from 43.00 dollars to 51.60 dollars for a 20-minute care coordination session), the company would see a Value on Investment (VOI) which requires quit a commitment to measuring adequately. These downstream results must be captured and considered equally important when leveraging value. These activities must be across one's enterprise and benchmarked with ER avoidance, readmissions avoidance, prevention of adverse outcomes during transitions of care, closing care gaps, engagement of high risk and utilizers of care, and preventive quality metrics. You must define your population, evaluate your contracts as you partner with payors, standardize systems of care and workflows, measure with scorecards, and use this data to leverage value. Therefore, this return stems largely from a "whole-system" approach to a novel service that does not just hinge on reducing unnecessary, unwanted readmissions to hospitals.

Because integrated care is a relatively new model for providing healthcare, insurance companies will understandably need to be convinced of its efficacy. And the suggestion that you should take on the task of reforming the daunting payment barriers in our healthcare system may make you want to throw this book at the wall. But the top physicians in the country count themselves as being among those who have influence over these systemic payment barriers.

"The ACP recommends that public and private health insurance payers, policymakers, and primary care and behavioral healthcare professionals work toward removing payment barriers that impede behavioral health and primary care integration," according to the ACP's Public Policy Committee. "Stakeholders should also ensure the availability of adequate financial resources to support the practice infrastructure required to effectively provide such care."

Use the Codes

The simplest task to take on payment barriers is to just use the codes. But to take advantage of an opportunity to cover care coordination services, some training is usually required of the care coordinators and physicians. That is because some of these codes, such as coordinated care or case management, are commonly buried in the medical provider list, resulting in infrequent utilization.

Take the CPT code for the care manager as an example. Using this code, you could hire a care manager to make calls to the patient twice a month, for 20 minutes, collecting data about their progress, use that data for the next time they come to an on-site, or a telehealth visit. Some organizations have reallocated resources by having medical assistants, case managers, and mental health specialists fulfill these positions. Staff are generally well prepared to deliver this care and enjoy the newfound role of connecting between official appointments as they are actively providing assessment and interventions.

Advocate for Patients

Individual providers may not have the opportunity to talk on the phone with health insurance executives, but they can step up their coordination with insurance carriers and may be required to manage appeals when coverage is denied. This work can be frustrating. And, until the insurance industry recognizes the financial benefit of integrated care, many of the conversations will be dead ends. But when you do succeed, it serves as an invaluable form of advocacy on behalf of the patient.

Insurance companies have been reluctant to pay for SUD treatment in the past, particularly in the early stages of the disease. The tendency was to wait until the patient hit bottom before paying for care—or only approving lower levels of care.

Compare this to somatic illness and injury. If you present at the ER with bad chest pains, you will be brought in immediately for tests—you may even be admitted for an inpatient stay that very day. But if you present at the ER with drug addiction, at most you will be prescribed an outpatient medication-assisted therapy, which would reduce cravings for the substance.

At a lower level of integration, the ER provider would just give them a referral. If you are even that fortunate, then you must be in a provider institution that has started the earliest stages of integrated care. In many places, you may get nothing but a printout with a list of community addiction resources. That may be the case even if you came in with an overdose. That may be the case even if your addiction has advanced to the point where you are committing violent crimes, being coerced into sex work, or losing your home. This tragic phenomenon has resulted in poor outcomes and negligence from the healthcare systems including behavioral healthcare in most cases. According to the HEDIS data set, nearly a third (30.3%) of patients do not complete a single outpatient visit in the first 30 days after inpatient behavioral health care in the United States (National Committee for Quality Assurance, 2017).

However, I am seeing some hopeful signs. Increased communication between care providers and the insurance industry has convinced many insurance companies that a much more cost-effective approach is to pay for early intervention, with the hopes of preventing more expensive treatment later.

This is a part of the insurance industry's shift to a focus on patient wellness in real-time and harm reduction while providing services that maintain health as a way of avoiding more costly procedures to restore health. And if you are lucky enough to be coordinating with a payer like this, then your job is much easier.

Advocating for individual patients' care coverage with insurance companies requires resources and investments. But it is also critical to help patients advocate for themselves. Dedicating staff to support patients in understanding their insurance programs and responsibilities increases care possibilities. For example, by promoting this model of care which includes assessing pain, one's range of physical motion, status of one's disease state, whether the existence of co-occurring disorders is present, and other process addictions patients become empowered and demand ways of improving their mental and physical health. This results in advocacy across specialties which could eventually be quantified as "What are you willing to pay for a year of healthy life?" mandate of payors.

Advocate for Yourself

Another reason for the under-utilization of billing codes related to care management is that they are reimbursed at such low rates. One of the most important interactions a healthcare business leader can have with an insurance carrier is simply to renegotiate the rates with commercial payers.

Your system or practice should demand better reimbursement for care management and other services tied to integrated care. In these negotiations, two tactics are a foundation for success: Illustrating the financial benefit for the payer and illustrating your own institution's fidelity in concrete metrics.

Using those two tactics, you should at least be able to get reimbursement rates that are within the range of Medicaid and Medicare standards. Provider institutions often settle for less than the government rates, which is unacceptable. A practice built on that level of reimbursement is not a sustainable model for delivering care.

For example, let us revisit the Current Procedural Terminology (CPT) code for a care manager. Most private insurance companies will pay around $25 for this 20-minute service. But Medicaid and Medicare will pay $46 for that code. So, at a minimum, you need to walk away with at least what the government is valuing this service at and paying. That rate is a foundation for hiring somebody to contact three patients in an hour to get this done.

Organizational Strategies

Healthcare systems and practices must also take organizational approaches to address payment barriers. Implemented integrated care is, in and of itself, a way to reduce payment barriers.

Most insurance limits the amount they will pay for a particular patient. So, coordination done properly can help ensure that the primary and pressing needs are covered first. Otherwise, patients may find themselves reaching the end of covered care while still having to address ancillary/minor issues instead of the primary or main problem. In an ideal world, this would not be an issue, but the reality of limited resources makes this avenue of communication and prioritization a necessity requiring expertise. In this way, integrated care reduces out-of-pocket costs for individual patients but still must overcome barriers.

Capitated payment models can provide insurers with an increase in reimbursement to cover treatment as they focus on a fee Per Member Per Month (PMPM) and these models can encourage providers to offer an array of services that improve outcomes. Some of these payment approaches are flat rates, some are adjusted for case-mix and geography-based, and some focus on the provider "level of care" when determining reimbursement. Therefore, the two factors are the number of services provided or utilized and the price or cost of these services. For example, the number of conditions an individual has that requires care, the expected number of episodes per condition, the type of service per episode and the processes involved, and the cost per process. These lead to an estimated cost which places the payer and provider at risk. This model requires close monitoring and expedited negotiations among all stakeholders (Hackbarth, 2015).

And in the end, the organization should be committed to providing best practices regardless of reimbursement models as both allow for these services to be offered which are included in this model of whole health. Healthcare groups that provide the best integrated care have shown a dedication to financing such care, whether incremental effect, i.e., inclusive of more evidenced-based services or incremental cost, i.e., more providers to deliver the services.

Managing internal finances is also key. Remember that the standards of care include being accountable to the payers, which are measured by payors who monitor their members and beneficiary's experience, quality of service, cost, utilization and affordability, customers other than members, market share of providers, network leverage, and regulations adherence. So organizational culture must be able to assess their strengths and weaknesses, identify gaps in one's model, respond to data analytics, and have continued engagement with patients. This will make insurance carriers more willing to cover services within your organization generally.

References

Centers for Disease Control and Prevention. (2020). *Prescription opioid overdose data*. Retrieved from https://www.cdc.gov/drugoverdose/data/overdose.html

Hackbarth, N. S. (2015). Financing integrated care for adults with serious mental illness in community mental health centers: An overview of program components, funding environments, and financing barriers. Working paper RAND Health.

8 Communication

The primary responsibility of healthcare staff is to make sure all facets of patients' health are being treated. This task is, of course, at the core of integrated care as well.

Whole person care is facilitated by an organizational culture that encourages interdisciplinary collaboration. It is crucial for each team member to not only play their role, but also the roles of others. They should have an appreciation of how each person's specialty contributes to the patient's health.

Other than direct interactions with patients, communication between team members is the most important component of integrated care. AHRQ's guidebook for integrated care notes that communication among staff can also be the key to de-escalating conflicts between providers and patients.

Communication beyond the organization is important too. Making sure the message one sends is the message being received as an organization leads to one's brand as a thought leader in the industry.

Some of this improved communication results from the care model itself. When care is delivered by a highly collaborative team, patient needs are less likely to drop off the radar. In addition, when a pediatrician requests an ADHD assessment from a BHP colleague down the hall, it inevitably improves the pediatrician's understanding of what is being assessed, which feeds back into better decision-making about prescriptions for the patient. The proximity improves communication by default.

Frequency also improves communication. Consider a specialist who sees a patient every two months. Is it ideal to rely entirely on the patient's self-report of how things have been going since the last appointment?

Instead, imagine that care management has been occurring throughout that time. The physician has 80 minutes of data over that period because some quick assessments were done and some instruments were deployed. That synopsis provides a much clearer picture. This improved communication is a key factor in the success of integrated care implementations.

But it is not sufficient to rely on the organic communication improvements that result from the implementation of the care model. Leaders must promote communication through both active and passive methods.

DOI: 10.4324/9781003128571-8

Active Promotion of Communication

Even in integrated care, interdisciplinary collaboration and training should be actively encouraged. This includes soliciting input from a number of specialties. Those providing inputs need to be open about their areas of expertise and the limits of their knowledge, as well as their comfort level in addressing particular issues.

Leadership also needs to ensure that a clear description of the mission and vision is communicated to applicants. And, once new staff comes on board, their orientation should include thorough training about the culture of integrated care within the company.

This teamwork concept can be seen in the Six C's model (Salas, 2013) for interprofessional education, which can serve as a framework for care delivery:

1. Cooperation
2. Communication
3. Conflict
4. Coordination
5. Coaching
6. Cognitive

The importance of Cooperation stems from its ability to provide trust and safety for all with a shared experience. This requires the ability of each member to be agile in all situations and always have the focus on the needs of the individual receiving care.

Clear communication involves making sure the sender and receiver are engaged in a reciprocal process. When you can anticipate what another care team member is going to need to know, you can go ahead and give them the information before they have to ask. In this way, that reciprocal process builds anticipation skills, which enhances efficiencies.

Healthy Conflict can occur in the context of tasks, relationships, or processes within a team. It often restores fairness and effectiveness while improving critical thinking skills. The need to manage in all directions by holding any member accountable and responsible in a respectful manner solidifies inclusiveness.

The ability to practice coordination transforms teams by orchestrating resources into outcomes. Everyone recognizes the importance of their contribution which improves efficiencies. This becomes fluid and natural while benefiting all.

The need to have leadership in the form of coaching sets directional goals where individuals take turns leading and following. All can participate in managing each other vertically and laterally at times throughout the lifespan of the care team, even if their time as a team is only for the day.

Finally, the cognitive aspect of the Six C's model requires team members to have shared mental models and values for care deliverables. Every member of the team should understand the team's workflows. The values (e.g., the quality of care strived for and the preferred treatments for certain conditions) should be explicit and well-understood. This allows the team to manage crises, ruptures, and successes in a dynamic fashion with self-corrective skills, as interdisciplinary training is assimilated.

The "NICELY DONE" mnemonic may be helpful for training staff who are new to the type of communication that integrated care requires (Raney, 2017):

- To summarize these strategies, one must consider the Nicely: Which builds trust and rapport
- D: Diagnosing and being open to other team voices throughout the care delivery
- O: Offer concise feedback and suggestions when communicating
- N: Next steps and "if then" scenarios as anticipatory guidance for alternative/critical thinking
- E: Continuously educate the patient and care team members, which embraces inclusion

This welcoming tone can be refreshing as the intensity/complexity of these conditions warrants collaboration.

Promoting Communication by Design

Another set of practices centers on building structures that passively promote communication. These can include physical structures or organizational structures. Developed protocols and a regular meeting structure can tailor the workflow to favor integration.

Organizational charts can also help promote integrated care. Clearly defined roles and responsibilities help staff understand their part in providing care. It can also increase staff flexibility because the staff is aware of the functions they need to perform when they are asked to work outside their area of specialization.

And instead of the separation between leadership and staff, managers and directors need to be involved in clinical practice. This allows them to remain informed about how care is being provided, to stay up to date on developments in the field, and to model integrated care for others.

The shadowing of care providers in fields other than their own is a good way to educate new hires about the roles of other specialists within the practice. This leads to familiarity across the systems of care with an adaptation of language, professionalism, and reduces burnout.

Building a meeting structure that facilitates collaboration is another critical way to passively facilitate communication. These meetings take a number of different forms. This section expands on the two formal forms of communication: Team meetings and huddles.

Regular staff meetings are for discussion of issues related to both the treatment of patients and the process of collaborative care. Team/staff meetings involve the entire team and take place at regular intervals.

These meetings have two goals. The first is the sharing of patient information and planning for treatment. Everyone on the team is brought up to speed on how each patient is progressing. Providers also have the chance to ask questions about care in order to make better decisions concerning formulating or changing treatment plans. They can explore any new barriers that could impact successful progress, new diagnoses, or plans for family therapy. It is also a chance to offer input on treatment.

The second goal of staff meetings is the improvement of team processes. These gatherings are the time to address and resolve any problems with the process itself, including conflicts and inefficiencies.

Huddles, reports, and staffings are much more frequent, of shorter duration, and more focused. They are not the appropriate venue for the discussion of process issues, which are better addressed at team and staff meetings or supervision.

Huddles may occur prior to and following patient/staff meetings, as providers gather briefly to stay up to date on the patient's progress, receive input that can help make treatment decisions, plan for treatment and handoffs between providers, consult quickly with specialists.

Huddles usually happen at least once a day. Most teams prefer to do once-daily huddles at the beginning of the day, although others have found different times throughout the day work as well.

The purpose of the daily huddle is the discussion of immediate patient needs, usually for patients who will be seen that same day and who are new to the system. Once-daily huddles quickly run through a discussion of all patients to be seen that day. This brings each team member up to date on progress. Each team has a chance to provide input with regard to diagnosis, assessment, and treatment. A patient's overall health is considered, and a plan is created based on the input of both mental and physical care providers. The consultation also allows providers to discuss difficult issues that may hinder the provision of care or hamper patient follow-through.

Because huddles are intended to provide short summaries for—at times—a large number of patients, it is important that providers learn to present their information in a succinct fashion. While medical doctors are familiar with such summaries because of their ability to deal with quantifiable elements such as patient vital signs, BHPs may need some practice and guidance to be able to provide the needed information in a short time.

The SBAR approach to communication has been shown to be useful in such a setting. Originally developed as a way for submarine personnel to communicate quickly and accurately, it has become a standard approach for the exchange of information in critical situations (Dunsford, 2009). Both The Joint Commission and the Institute for Healthcare Improvement endorse the SBAR as a form of structured communication (Johnson, 2013). The steps are as follows:

- Situation: A concise summary of the issue
- Background: A brief statement of relevant history
- Assessment: An analysis and diagnosis
- Recommendation: A suggested course of action

Each step should take no more than five to ten seconds, allowing the entire case to be summarized in thirty seconds. This facilitates a huddle where dozens of patients need to be discussed in a short period of time. Although the rubric may seem confining at first, providers who use the method regularly soon find that it helps them focus their ideas and even makes it easier to prepare for the huddle.

In addition to these formal meetings and huddles, ad hoc consultations and informal tête-à-têtes take place on a regular basis.

Communicating with others in the network is also a key to integrated health. Consultations with specialties outside the practice allow providers to decide on treatment plans that are beyond their area of expertise and make referrals for cases they cannot handle.

The physical spaces of the practice can also be arranged to promote integrated care. Staff should be the lead when new design and technology are being considered. A survey found that successful clinics frequently had shared workspaces that facilitated communication, collaboration, and coordination. Individual examination rooms were maintained for privacy, but clinicians often worked in open spaces as a team when they were not with patients. The power of space for both care staff and patients consuming care has developed with attention to exteriors, the layout of flow, interior finishes, and natural light. This has led to a resurgence of companies representing health architecture (BD+C, 2017).

References

BD+C. (2017, August 29). *Top 125 healthcare architecture firms*. Retrieved from BDC Network: https://www.bdcnetwork.com/top-125-healthcare-architecture-firms

Dunsford, J. (2009). Structured communication: Improving patient safety with SBAR. *Nursing for Women's Health, 13*(5), 384–390. doi: 10.1111/j.1751-486X.2009.01456.x

Johnson, M. (2013, November 19). *SBAR: A powerful tool to help improve communication*. Retrieved from The Joint Commission Blog: https://www.

jointcommission.org/resources/news-and-multimedia/blogs/at-home-with-the-joint-commission/2013/11/sbar--a-powerful-tool-to-help-improve-communication/

Raney, L. E. (2017). *Integrated care: A guide for effective implementation.* Washington, DC: American Psychiatric Association Publishing.

Salas, E. L. (2013). On being a team player: Evidence-based heuristic for teamwork in interprofessional education. *Medical Science Educator, 23*(3 Suppl.), 524–531.

9 Measurement-Based Care

Thinking back to my time at Pine Grove, it is clear that much of the success of that organization stemmed from CEO Vicky Pevsner's commitment to both innovation and collaboration. She surrounded herself with a talent ladened clinical and executive team to execute her vision which sustains the organization to this day. For me though, after 12 years of providing leadership by collaborating with gifted clinicians, designing industry-leading programs, supervising clinicians, acquiring talent, evaluating programs for strategic planning, researching outcomes, and publishing the results, a third major career opportunity presented itself.

I was given the chance to restructure a program from the ground up, for the second time, with the goal of providing integrative care. Lakeview Health was a large primary substance use disorder (SUD) facility in Jacksonville, Florida. Lakeview provided multiple levels of care (e.g., medical detoxification, inpatient care, residential, partial hospitalization, and intensive outpatient care). But they needed more specialization—and, at the same time, more collaboration. They needed someone to assess the organization's deliverables, lead innovative initiatives, provide translation between the clinical and business teams, examine policies and procedures to delineate how patient care was being provided, recruit talent, and partner both within the organization and within the treatment industry.

So, in June 2015, I moved to the Sunshine State. When I arrived, I found a program that again was providing good foundational addiction treatment but lacked advanced collaboration systems and integrated services. They had tremendous leadership, resources, and a commitment to high standards, but little clinical expertise.

I was able to begin to create a collaborative system of healthcare that treated the complex causes of addiction and expanded the probability of appropriately treating co-occurring disorders. I led the development and implementation of plans for provision of patient care services. By building teams, guiding leadership, developing a vision for staff to buy in, and implementing a 30-day, 60-day, 90-day inclusive assessment, the goals, and objectives focused on patient care being at the center of this

DOI: 10.4324/9781003128571-9

collaborative care model. Small victories were celebrated while action-oriented strategies were mapped out and executed.

This was not "business as usual." Our intense focus on evaluation, assessment, and treatment reflected a commitment to measurement-based care (MBC). The integrated care facility served as a "learning organization." There are two sides to this.

The first is that the organization is a place where learning is encouraged and partnerships with higher learning institutions allow for ongoing innovation. Leadership needs to be open to staff members taking risks to try new approaches, and they must also be tolerant of mistakes. This allows practitioners to explore new ways to engage patients without fear of organizational repercussions. Performance goals, instead of adherence to traditional practices, should be the measure of how successful each approach really is. And care must be agile.

But being a learning organization does not just mean being a place where individual professionals learn. The second side to this aspect is being an organization that itself learns from its own performance, as well as teaches these lessons to other provider institutions. In integrated care, the collecting of information about patient care is an important responsibility of the staff.

Learning organizations are committed to ongoing quality improvement, both through investment in human capital and through constant performance assessment. Ongoing improvement means a measurement-based approach to gauging the effectiveness of treatment and processes. The importance of MBC has been advocated in recent years, and the Joint Commission made such data a requirement for accreditation of behavioral health providers starting in January 2018 (Fortney, 2015).

MBC allows practices to gauge which providers and care systems are effective and which need to improve their approach. The data collected during MBC also provides a baseline for program evaluation, needs assessments, client satisfaction evaluations, and outcome studies during and following treatment.

Although the behavioral health field has made strides in the adoption of quantitative evidence-based or data-driven practices, it still lags behind the medical field. Medical doctors have long made use of clinical trials to determine the effectiveness of medications. They also track patient outcomes to measure the effectiveness of particular therapies. Those practices that meet certain criteria for efficacy are continued, while those for which the data do not show improvement are modified or abandoned.

The field of behavioral health and addiction treatment has not always adhered as closely to the requirements for evidence-based care. Evidence-based practices are available, including Cognitive Behavioral Therapy, Dialectical Behavior Therapy, and Exposure Therapy. And scientifically based resources are available on SAMHSA's Evidence-Based Practices Resource Center. Yet the field of SUD treatment has a mixed record on evidence-based treatments. Access to treatment protocols, toolkits, resource guides, clinical practice guidelines, and other relevant science-based information inform those treatment centers who are careful to follow such modalities, while others use some methods for which evidence is lacking or inconclusive.

Fortunately, you can fix this problem in your own practice, as well as generate your own evidence to fuel continuous improvement. But it will require standardized screenings, good technology, interoperability in your information systems, and a commitment to using these protocols and technology for continuous improvement.

With these tactics in place, your center can achieve MBC, a critical aspect of integrated care. MBC is the practice of collecting patient data and using those data to develop a course of treatment. SAMHSA recognizes MBC as an evidence-based practice, and the Joint Commission—one of the two primary credentialing bodies for behavioral healthcare providers—began requiring MBC as part of its standards for accreditation in 2018 (Fortney, 2015).

The tracking of patient metrics refers to the collection of data from standardized screening tools such as PHQ-9 for depression, PCL-5 for post-traumatic stress, and GAD-7 for anxiety. These tools allow staff to record patient-reported symptoms on a numerical scale. Although the subjective nature of this reporting does not allow comparison between patients, it does allow staff to measure an individual patient's progress over time.

Almost all medical care providers use health information systems or electronic health records (EHR) that allow them to make patient records accessible across the practices. These systems can also provide information to other care centers when needed, as in the case of referrals. These records track the patients' progress and can monitor measurements across multiple vital signs, prescription patterns, unscheduled visits, etc.

In a fully integrated health home with a state-of-the-art EHR, all medical and behavioral information is recorded in a single system. This prevents patients from needlessly providing information multiple times to multiple providers. EHRs provide a single repository for data on a patient, making it easier for doctors and clinicians to find the information they need. It also allows doctors and counselors to monitor patients' progress and address any treatment plans that have stalled. EHRs can provide support for scheduling, collaboration, and screening.

Why do we do so much screening in integrated care? Patient metrics are tracked for three primary purposes. The first is to allow the provision of MBC. The data can provide a gauge of how the treatment is progressing or indicate when a patient's progress has stalled.

The second reason for tracking patient metrics is that it makes available an empirical basis for evaluating the care provided by individual practitioners or facilities. By looking at the progress of all patients being treated for specific problems, organizations can determine which practitioners are providing care that consistently leads to patient improvement. They can also identify those staff who may need to adjust their approaches. This is a way to realize the commitment to continual improvement and reduce the probability of health disparities that is part of the integrated care model.

Finally, patient tracking allows organizations to demonstrate their results. Outcome studies can use these data as a basis for showing their effectiveness in treating specific conditions. The need to provide evidence of effective treatments is becoming critical. Insurance plans often consider such evidence when deciding what types of behavioral health treatments to cover (America's Health Insurance Plans, 2016). The credibility and quality metrics are imperative as some patients are "superutilizers" of the healthcare system. These patients need a flexible and personalized approach to care which is not conducive to some reimbursement models. Providers will have a difficult time with managed care entities that use value-based metrics for reimbursement if they do not adopt emerging technologies (e.g., personal device monitoring, transportation for wellness services, destigmatized environments) and new science when providing services as recidivism rates will be compromised.

Standardized Screenings

Another important commitment by an organization that aims to render state-of-the-art care is to require universal comprehensive screening of all patients. It increases the comfort level of care providers when they know what needs to be intervened on to maximize results. In addition to treating issues raised by the patient, the staff must administer screening instruments to detect additional health problems (e.g., pain disorders, eating disorders, the severity of the trauma, and sexual disorders). This gives providers confidence in triaging and delivering the care they are leading. This has led specifically to the identification and management of chronic disease states that may otherwise go undetected.

Universal screening also promotes a willingness to be an active approach which patients prefer. It opens treatment team members to possibilities of contributing variables and removes barriers to skill development and comprehensive yet personalized treatment plans. Practitioners feel a stronger sense of contribution. This is because comprehensive screening requires all appropriate clinicians, not just the physician or primary BHP, to administer the instruments. Having care team members rely on each other to measure functionality in each patient clarifies treatment pathways, increases cultural competencies, enhances feedback loops within organizations, and promotes egalitarian interdisciplinary care being provided by all staff. In addition, accountability improves when we know others are involved in our work.

Triage is an important part of the assessment process because it allows providers to address mental health issues using a stepped-care approach. Triage includes determining whether an issue is acute or chronic and what level of care is required. The ability to triage conditions can increase exponentially with multiple providers while expanding and stretching professionals, which forces a process of "mentalizing." This perceiving and interpreting a patient's needs by numerous practitioners allows for a deeper and richer understanding of their desires, feelings, beliefs, goals, purpose, and reasons for their struggles. It encourages practitioners to see patients from the inside while identifying their inherent strengths.

Therefore, PCPs must be cross-trained to screen for and identify behavioral health conditions and SUDs. These screenings often include such mental health assessments as Kessler 10 (K-10) for psychological distress, the Patient Health Questionnaire 9 (PHQ-9) for depression, PTSD Checklist (PCL-5) for post-traumatic stress, and (GAD-7) for anxiety. The NIDA Modified ASSIST (NM ASSIST) (National Institute on Drug Abuse, 2019) is an instrument utilized for quick screenings and interventions for SUDs. The goal, of course, is to catch mental health and substance use problems as early as possible.

PCPs must also be aware of the treatment services available when problems are found. Behavioral health providers have a role in the process as well by providing ongoing consultation services to PCPs and by screening for medical conditions during SUD treatment.

Screenings should be customized to certain patient populations. For example, women who suffer from addiction are more likely to have had at least one past experience of major trauma when compared with the general population. That correlation strongly suggests that addressing trauma is important in treating patients with SUD and supports the inclusion of a good trauma inventory when addressing and treating medical conditions in this population. At the very least, all patients will have a brief screening. And, if the person scores high enough, you bump it up to a more formal trauma assessment.

One special issue that needs to be discussed in this context is the topic of physical contact. Touching is a general part of a physical exam. Within the context of behavioral health therapy, however, it is often discouraged and should always be clearly communicated if required (Patterson, 2016). PCPs and BHPs will need to discuss with specific patients before exams to determine whether any issues are present that would make physical contact contraindicated. For example, a woman who has experienced sexual trauma may be understandably wary about touch and may be supported by a chaperone during an exam, even in a medical setting. Other patients may be dealing with body image issues/body dysmorphic disorder or other problems that would affect their willingness to submit to an exam. Collaboration between PCPs and BHPs is vital to ensuring that patients receive the physical healthcare they need in a way that does not further traumatize them (Center for Substance Abuse Treatment, 2014). So, having a BHP or nurse who has a rapport with the patient in the exam is advantageous.

In different specialized populations, you are going to have to do different types of assessments. With adolescents, you need to have an ADHD assessment in place or the Child and Adolescent Behavior Assessment (CABA-Y). With geriatric patients, you may have to do more of a neurocognitive assessment with a Montreal Cognitive Assessment (MoCA) which is a brief 10-minute cognitive screen to detect mild impairment in order to sort SUDs from the type of neurological issues that are more common among seniors. So, screenings should be uniform to the degree appropriate, with some customization to the needs of particular populations.

Following standardized workflows increases patient access to mental health services, particularly when multiple pathways (for example, warm handoffs, consultations) can lead patients into a relationship with behavioral health specialists. These set workflows can also facilitate communication between specialists, especially when pre-visit meetings and huddles are scheduled to discuss patient needs and debriefing meetings allow observations to be shared post-visit.

Data Sharing

Standardized screenings generate volumes of incredibly helpful data—but how do you glean insights from it? How do you share it with other members of the care team? That is where technology systems come in.

Back in the mid-80s, only a small group of Americans were aware of Bill Gates, and an even smaller group grasped his vision for the personal computer. Integrated care was just starting to gain some traction in small pockets of healthcare around the world. And the preferred medium for collecting patient information was paper.

Yes, paper. They were notebooks. We called them registries, pass down reports, communication logs, etc. It is hard for today's professionals in training to imagine. But we carried around objects made entirely of paper, bound by glue or thread or a metal spiral. We wrote down notes about the patient's progress, and to share this information with other members of the care team, we literally placed it in their hands.

Not only was sharing data a challenge, but it was also difficult to extrapolate meaning and progress from the registries. Now, with a good EHR and an optimized approach to using technology, these silos are breaking down. And in addition, we can now extrapolate and monitor key performance indicators. We can track how much time a person spends in remission from a SUD, what descriptive words are used to indicate the amount of empathy a physician expresses, and many other measurements of progress. The potential is amazing.

And yet, while technology in healthcare has promised to render better, faster, more accurate care delivery services, the innovation curve has yet to provide the windfall expected at this time. A major shortcoming in the systems developed thus far is a lack of interoperability.

Technology is at the heart of integrated care.

Technology for the Care Coordination Model
By Neal Tilghman, MPA and Andy Fosnacht, MS

As the healthcare industry continues to shift from fee-for-service to alternative payment models, organizations need to be data driven and have the ability to treat the whole person. Integrated care models address behavioral, addiction and physical health aspects of an individual. Understanding all aspects of an individual in treatment is why health IT matters. The concept of whole-person care is not new to human services, but we have not had the technology to adequately support integrated approaches to care until now.

A major step in the direction of integrated care began during the late 80s with the creation of Federally Qualified Health Centers (FQHC). The purpose of the FQHC initiative was to provide underserved populations with one physical location where several of their healthcare needs could be met. Marrying dentistry, behavioral health, and primary care together was a revolutionary idea and people started to see different determinants, and the outcomes thereof, as linked. One's physical health can affect their mental health and addiction and conversely. But as common sense as this idea sounds our journey is not yet complete.

In the 80s, FQHC's were a response to a poverty crisis; now we have an opioid crisis, the impacts of a pandemic, and a continued trend of increased service demand, so the need to serve a population as all determinants is critical. For example, SUDs are among the top six health conditions affecting Americans today. In 2018, more than 10.3 million people misused prescription opioids, while 2 million people had an opioid use disorder (OUD). Overall, more than 130 people die every day—47,600 people a year—from opioid overdoses. In addition to the projected increase in opioid related deaths, there are also an increased number of individuals showing up in the emergency department (ED) for opioid-related care. From July 2016 to September 2017, ED visits for opioid overdoses increased by 30%. Unfortunately, not all EDs are equipped to treat individuals effectively and efficiently with an OUD because oftentimes they do not have dedicated behavioral health and addiction providers on staff to address their needs. In fact, only 17% of emergency physicians reported having a psychiatrist on call to respond to psychiatric emergencies in the ED.

Technology supporting the original mission of the FQHC program (integrated care) to treat the whole person has never been more important. Integrated care systems promote whole-person care by providing a single solution for use in both primary care and behavioral health clinics. As a result, primary care and behavioral health providers share the same medication list, problem list, and treatment history. A single patient record is built to provide the best possible care. Integrated care systems or platforms include an EHR with a robust set of features that support the care delivery models of an organization. No doubt we have made much progress since the late 1980s, but we now need to look beyond the EHR. Integrated care solutions must provide technology that is complementary or extends the features found in the traditional EHR such as analytics, mobile solutions, interoperability, patient engagement, and remote patient supports. The below graphic provides the foundation for a checklist that organizations might utilize when developing "self-assessment" tools and strategies for integrated care models, i.e., care coordination.

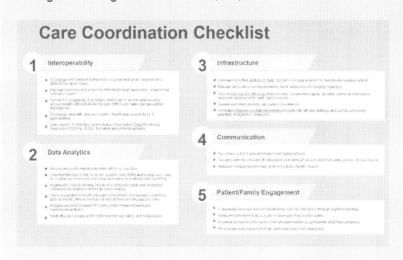

So how can we more favorably influence not just the population being served, but also the peripheral providers that are co-serving that population? The first component for making decisions about our own health is based on data. Data is integral to truly understand the makeup and health of an individual patient, the health of a population as well as the "health" of the organization. The better the analytics tool, the better the data, the more actionable that data becomes. A primary role of a robust analytics platform is to transition an organization from a reactive model to a predictive model. We have an opportunity to deliver care and deliver interventions beyond how we have delivered historically. There are emerging technologies that utilize wearables and "apps" to obtain real-time feedback of patient data that can then alert when a patient might be at a heightened risk of relapse, suicide, or even heightened risk of overdose. By utilizing machine learning approaches to develop algorithms for predicting a potentially risky behavior. This technology is impactful primarily in that it has the potential to save a life by averting an overdose but also it is a risk mitigation and cost-saving tool. It is in the best interest of an organization to keep the patient healthy and out of the ED.

To advance care coordination, an organization needs access to data regarding the populations that have been entrusted to their care; understanding the social determinant profile of each population, how clinical care relates to financial health, what programs are put in place post-discharge with numbers of touches and interactions, and how all that relates to recidivism, etc. The only way to investigate all of those items is with good data and the ability to securely share and exchange data. Data analytics and interoperability need to be viewed as symbiotic in that they are not mutually exclusive.

Once you start to understand your internal needs, you can better communicate with other providers on the unique needs of your population, share data and provide informed care across the continuum. Which of course means needing the appropriate communications tools. The addiction space has long been stymied with an inability or hesitancy to share data, despite many HIPAA compliant data sharing tools having been available for years. Several decades ago, 42 CFR Part 2 regulations were warranted and needed, but it has also helped created some of the fragmentation and roadblocks to achieving integrated care. However, some healthcare IT leaders, in anticipation of market demands, policy shifts and advances in technology, incorporated logic into their data sharing tools that account for the ability to share data across organizations in a 42 CFR Part 2 compliant manner utilizing explicit consent as opposed to general consent. So, as a consumer one can individually identify providers with which to share data and only release information to those providers. Furthermore, the market is being spurred to better interoperability through regulatory forces like the Trusted Exchange Framework and Common Agreement being implemented by the Office of the National Coordinator. This means, if you were once in an interoperability desert, the entire country is being turned into an oasis, even going as far as to punish those that would not share data through mechanisms like the Information Blocking Rule.

Once you have data sharing mechanisms in place, it does not stop at the provider-to-provider model. The regulatory climate is increasingly incorporating the individual (patient) into the model. Organizations that have robust consumer engagement strategies in the near term will far outshine their competitors and be able to negotiate better rates due to better outcomes.

Prior to 2020, the virtual healthcare landscape was growing at a steady pace, but in a post-2020 healthcare world, the choice is expected as to how individual patients receive their healthcare. Virtual engagement is just expected as one of the several choices as to how care is delivered. Virtual service delivery through telehealth, automated appointment reminders, and mobile health platforms are how consumers expect to be engaged. Initial data is supporting the benefits and importance of virtual service delivery. For example, appointment kept rates skyrocketed, while session time lowered allowing for greater visit volume. Furthermore, mobile consumer engagement platforms will continue to pave the way for not just how providers engage with consumers but how we can change behavior and continue to advance care coordination.

There are numerous opportunities and emerging technology that will continue to enhance care coordination, our ability to treat the whole person and deliver interventions real-time. We have an opportunity to capitalize upon research conducted by other industries. In 2019, the fast food industry experimented with the concept of geo-conquesting and it has incredibly interesting implications in the healthcare market. For example, consumers who downloaded the Burger King app would be prompted with a special, limited time offer for a Whopper if they entered into geo-fenced Mcdonald's location. This was intended to change the behavior of the consumer and it worked! Now, imagine an individual struggling with addiction with a consumer engagement app downloaded that prompts them with a push notification if they enter an establishment geo-fenced as a bar.

"We noticed you may be in an area that may be a trigger for you. Would you like to talk to someone?" If yes, all the individual needs to do is click a button where they are routed to a virtual session with an available provider or peer support specialist.

We are at a perfect nexus of technological advancement, regulatory incentive, and cultural adoption in which healthcare can move to be proactive rather than reactive, and capitalizing on these new trends will be vital as we provide care in the wake of an opioid crisis and a global pandemic.

In the aspect of integrated care implementation, interoperability comes first. That is because it is required to connect and exchange information while managing access to state-of-the-art care. Interoperability plays an essential role in allowing providers to integrate multiple influences on the patient's disease state or risk at the point of care. It enables smooth referrals and data-sharing with payers, pharmacies, and other stakeholders that are so essential to a good patient experience.

Organizations need to configure their EHR systems to support this essential collaboration. It is one of the hallmarks of fully integrated care for Levels 5 and 6 in SAMHSA's rubric, which we will explore in Chapter 12, Coordinated Care on a Spectrum. Implementing technology that supports collaboration aligns with the commitment to MBC that is part of the integrated care model, and it enables the goal of continuous improvement by indicating which care providers have acceptable outcomes and which need to adjust their approach for value-based delivery. The ability to provide real-time data analytics should guide the care being assigned. For example, we identified the increased risk for incomplete treatment by generating an internal risk-assessment scale which was developed using variables that predicted patient engagement. Also, we discovered specific substances of use and days of remission as in determining risk of administrative or against medical advice discharges. These findings guided our interventions with these individuals, their families, and employers. If we had ignored these data points, we would have been providing a disservice as once you collect data you are obligated ethically to assist individuals by sharing decision making.

These authors described the typical a seven-step process to effective EHR implementation:

1. Identifying the objectives and selecting the right vendor
2. Establishing a steering committee and well-rounded multi-disciplinary team

3. Assessing the organization's current operations, workflows, and clinical documentation procedures
4. Complete a system installation, configuration, and thorough testing
5. Develop training materials and facilitate staff training
6. System "go live"
7. Evaluate system performance and leverage the EHR capabilities over time

This checklist can be used to create cross-departmental technology while integrating it into management systems and capturing metrics for decision making.

Clinicians should develop appropriate documentation procedures to record and communicate patient information to others within the organization. Using EHR templates with data fields ensures that information is captured in qualitative and quantitative ways. BHPs who are accustomed to using a narrative style to describe patient progress may need to modify their record keeping to present information in a way that is more familiar to physicians and other medical providers.

Continuous Improvement

EHRs are not just for tracking patient-level data. They also provide support for organizational needs, such as key performance indicators and revenue cycle management. Integrated care also includes fidelity as measurements of interventions are available within an EHR.

In addition, given the value-based care milieu, leaders must have a conduit to manage cost, care, and outcomes across episodes of care while being able to track referrals, intake data, assessment/risk level, service billables/deliverables, insurance denial management, payment, and posting. This ensures the application of analytics for charters and other process improvements. These ultimately improve the quality of care with greater efficiencies while monitoring cost and leveraging with funders (Open Minds, n.d.).

Tilghman and Fosnacht say that once interoperability is in place, data analytics comes next. Data analytics provide a focus for execution while utilization of real-time data informs treatment/care decisions. A good system will allow you to produce and share key performance indicators in real-time, identify trends for decision support, and identify risk and care gaps in your patient population, among other capabilities.

But data analytics is not just for patient progress. As a result of experts, such as the ACP, calling for integrated care, there is now increased accountability and modeling of what integration requires (Mullin, 2019).

The ability to be accountable has taken over healthcare via value-based care, as metrics reveal the impact of interventions, determine reimbursement, and guide program offerings. Metrics have been deployed throughout the healthcare system as endless data points are available with the current EHRs. Although there has been disagreement on what are the necessary variables when considering impact and fidelity, enough findings point to a standard expected by funders and accreditation bodies.

The National Association of Addiction Treatment Providers has a guidebook with core competencies for the delivery of services (National Association of Addiction Treatment Providers, 2019). Their code of ethics is based on ASAM's Public Policy Statement; SAMHSA's definition of addiction; and ASAM's Treatment Placement Criteria coupled with the licensing and accreditation organizations which includes state agencies, Joint Commission, NCQA, COA, CQL, and CARF.

All of the treatment providers have spent years providing models of care and surveillance of quality whichis becoming overshadowed by the latest rating systems. These systems include Medicare and Medicaid Services (CMS) star ratings, Commonwealth Fund ratings, NAMI ratings, WHO ratings, Consumer Health Ratings, HealthGrades ratings, Leapfrog ratings, A.M. Best ratings, Shatterproof ratings, and consumer rating systems. Consumer systems include RateMD, vitals.com, Yelp, ZocDoc, CareDash, and Angie's List.

Needless to say, there are ample systems available and a recent NAATP outcomes study that has been much anticipated in the industry. This longitudinal pilot study of numerous treatment center from across the United States who have cultivated best practices revealed fairly successful outcomes for the 34% of participants who remained engaged throughout the survey while 46% of individuals treated reported continuous sobriety for the entire length of the assessment time frame. A majority of the participants had alcohol as the most common substance of use. Also of note, is the recent partnering of ASAM and CARF to certify treatment centers on standards of care for addiction treatment.

This criteria for evaluating care should include utility to determine the practical use of the standards, suitability and acceptability of feedback from an evaluation, sensitivity of real measurements, directness of feedback, non-reactivity to results, appropriateness for the population being served, and reliability and valid instruments utilized in measuring.

However, program outputs and outcomes are no longer sufficient to demonstrate the value of care delivery services. The capacity to scale up and generate evidence is linked to funding sources. Therefore, cost-effectiveness and cost-benefit analysis are both considered when determining the relative impact of these interventions, comparing benchmarks, projecting monetary terms, and monetizing one's services (Mukherjee, 2019). He stated, "in both for-profit and non-profit entities, funding is dependent on the ability to be translational of your data to match the mission of the organization."

Conclusion

The third item in Tilghman and Fosnacht's highlights infrastructure. An infrastructure platform that allows care providers to manage a patient's care across multiple systems—both internally and externally—is strengthened by designated case managers, recovery coaches, and alumni coordinators. This coordination is further enhanced by connecting patients to community resources, which can be the responsibility of your business development staff through referral placement. This outbound service allows individuals to be matched with the appropriate providers for continuity of care.

Tilghman and Fosnacht's fourth item is communication. Building this part of your system involves documenting everything on one platform, having secure communication among all care teams, and having the ability to view an individual's comprehensive health record. And finally, in integrated care, patients and family's engagement flourishes via digital technology. This allows risk to be mitigation by having quicker and more frequent access to providers, quality improvement with multiple touchpoints, increased assurance of bonding, and transparency for all stakeholders.

The structured data that EHRs collect can play a major role in the implementation of MBC. This integrated care model may be deployed when considering multiple processes within one's system and when faced with ruptures in workflows. Strategies include working towards understanding the identified problem, brainstorm by relevant stakeholders to generate creative objectives with a predicted desired impact and potential solutions, and followed by an assignment of a value for this impact. This often leads to feeling more confident when recommending your choice of strategy, policy, and intervention.

The approaches outlined in this chapter reflect an MBC delivery system with real-time feedback and change management (i.e., guiding teams which reduces tension, creating a vision to improve buy-in, celebrating victories, and continuing to remain focused). This involves identifying champions while maintaining ongoing monitoring which is the norm not the exception today.

References

America's Health Insurance Plans. (2016). Ensuring access to quality behavioral health care: Health plan examples (pp. 3–4). Retrieved from https://www.ahip.org/wp-content/uploads/2016/05/AccesstoBehavioralCare_May-2016.pdf

Center for Substance Abuse Treatment. (2014). *Trauma-informed care in behavioral health services*. Rockville, MD: Substance Abuse and Mental Health Services Administration.

Fortney, J. S. (2015). Fixing behavioral health care in America: A national call for measurement-based care in the delivery of behavioral health services. *The Kennedy Forum, revisions to behavioral health care outcome measures standard.* The Joint Commission. Retrieved from https://www.jointcommission.org/assets/1/6/Approved_BHC_outcome_meas_2018.pdf

Mukherjee, S. (2019, April). Personal communication.

Mullin, D. H. (2019). Measuring the integration of primary care and behavioral health services. *Health Services Research*, 54(2), 379–389.

National Association of Addiction Treatment Providers. (2019, April). *The addiction treatment provider quality assurance guidebook: A guide to the core competencies for the delivery of addiction treatment services.* Retrieved from https://www.naatp.org/sites/naatp.org/files/NAATP%20QA%20Guidebook%20Beta.pdf

National Institute on Drug Abuse. (2019, January 10). *Screening tools and prevention.* Retrieved from National Institute on Drug Abuse: Drugabuse.gov/nidamed-medical-health-professionals/tool-resources-your-practice/additional-screening-resources

Open Minds. (n.d.). Retrieved from EHR Best Practices: https://ehrbestpractices.org/

Patterson, F. (2016). *A touchy subject: The ethics of touching.* National Association for Alcoholism and Drug Abuse Counselors, the Association for Addiction. Retrieved from http://www.naadac.org/assets/2416/a_touchy_subject_the_ethics_of_touching_webinar_slides.pdf

10 Patient Experience

Imagine yourself in a dark jazz club. You are settling into your seat as you hear the first sounds of the band. They come on strong. Four musicians are all playing their instruments at the same time, but not necessarily in a way that your brain recognizes as harmonious.

What the players know is virtuosic improvisation just sounds like chaos to you. The band has a forceful presence that is too much for your brain to integrate.

It is only as the song progresses, and the musicians begin to take turns leading, that you can sort out what you are experiencing. Syncopation is readily utilized by the musicians as they enter and exit the mix with on and off-key riffs. This communication back and forth to each other conveys the direction, cadence, accents, and volume of their rhythm. Those audience members willing to listen intently may experience rhythmic distress and confusion. However, as you become more oriented to the music, you begin to get comfortable.

It took a moment, but now you can sort of understand what the musicians are doing. They are not playing different songs—they are playing off of each other. The measures begin to repeat themselves, and sensory knitting increases. You experience this as joy, awe, and groove.

This metaphor represents the struggles experienced in healthcare collaboration as patients must "trust the process" during overwhelming moments in their lives. In that situation, every cell in the patient's body is consumed with alertness. Sensory overload is the norm. Therefore, to be able to offer a path of clarification as a team of providers soothe the patient during their state of vulnerability is truly transformative and life-changing.

That is why the patient experience standard in integrated care is so high. The goals are to be flawless in communications, compassionate in diagnosing, strategic in care planning, agile in delivery, and vigilant in monitoring.

Fortunately, care that is truly integrated is easier to deliver in a way that is not overwhelming. In large part, that is because integrated care is suited to the individual and reflects the multidimensional determinants of health. But it is also because care management ensures follow-through

DOI: 10.4324/9781003128571-10

during care transitions, as well as because it includes active promotion of health literacy and a patient engagement that "meets them where they are." Their level of readiness for change depends on their perception of their own needs, their expectations of what is possible, their willingness to take risks, their social desirability, their entitlement level of having their needs met, and the available alternatives (Knight, 2014).

Engagement and Empowerment

One group of researchers (Poku, 2017) examined three non-healthcare companies with strong focuses on the customer: Ritz-Carlton Hotel Company, Disney, and Southwest Airlines. The researchers identified common themes and approaches of being tremendously focused on maximizing customer satisfaction through employee empowerment, innovative use of technology, and continuous improvement of day-to-day processes. The researchers propose adapting those methods to develop patient relationship management (PRM) in the healthcare context, to build trust and long-lasting patient-provider relationships, and to identify barriers to treatment compliance that can be solved collectively. This philosophy can be embraced by aftercare coordinators, recovery coaches, alumni coordinators (e.g., who assist with return visits), and case managers.

A promising area of focus today is the role of patient engagement in healthcare systems. Patients want to be active agents in their care, and engaged patients lead to better health outcomes. The literature is replete with examples of the positive effects of programs that increase patient involvement and engagement. For example, a cardiac center that took guidance from a patient advisory board saw a 46% reduction in heart failure readmission (Sharma, 2017).

Intensive outpatient programs (IOPs) meet multiple times per week and provide structured care as an element of a continuum. They were created to address patients' medical, social, and behavioral needs. However, even though these programs appear to be promising, they all struggle with patient engagement (Zulman, 2018).

Researchers who conducted a study of 12 IOPs in several settings, such as the VA and private healthcare, identified a wide variety of common barriers to patient engagement. Those barriers included individual unique physical, mental, and financial conditions, which can lead to differing access to social support structures, and a lack of coordination of care between different providers. To address barriers to patient engagement, the researchers proposed improving communication, trust, and counseling regarding problem-solving skills through the implementation of adequately staffed multi-disciplinary teams and a flexible, patient-centered organizational philosophy (Zulman, 2018).

Another study of 20 Medicaid patients with significant health issues corroborates that increasing patient engagement requires addressing the individual's unmet material and economic needs, as well as implementing an intensive organizational approach to the care required for these individuals (Komaromy, 2018).

Patients also want to be more engaged in their care, but they are often unable or unsure how to assert themselves which may be part of a broader mental health issue. Researchers interviewed VA patients receiving mental healthcare who were concerned about feeling inadequate, being judged or suspected in light of prior substance misuse history, or facing repercussions from providers (Eliacin, 2015).

Together, these studies paint a picture of key themes of the patient experience. Those themes include building trust and improving the quality of care and communication.

A final set of individual practices can help patients engage in their treatment. The determination of the course of care should be made with the desires of the patient in mind. What issues do they want to address first? Which is causing them the most distress? What are some unmet needs? What is their timeline for addressing these needs? Is there anything else they would like to let you know?

Because of the importance of the counselor–patient relationship, BHPs should be assured of working to build a rapport with their clients. Ways to enhance motivation for care compliance start with the relationship and problem recognition. Clinicians who just have a desire to assist can usually encourage patients to open up just by having a desire to help. Ongoing communication beyond the office visit may be appropriate depending on the situation and can impact the relationship between visits. Clinicians also need to clearly define their role with the patient. This may involve referring the client to a specialist outside the practice if their condition needs more intensive treatment.

Therefore, frequent communication is required and should not be redundant but relevant. All staff should work to deliver a consistent message to the patient about the treatment plan and available options. This is particularly important when addressing substance use disorders, where patients can sometimes seek to play clinicians against/off one another. And finally, only ask questions that you are committed to addressing.

Patient education is necessary. Wellness programming and other health supports should be provided by the integrated care practice. Through health literacy, integrated care empowers patients in a healthcare system that often makes them feel that they lack any control.

Another critical function of patient education is to address stigma. "The ACP recommends that all relevant stakeholders initiate programs to reduce the stigma associated with behavioral health," according to the ACP's Public Policy Committee (Crowley et al., 2015). "These programs need to address negative perceptions held by the general population and by many physicians and other healthcare professionals."

Providers should work to destigmatize the idea of mental healthcare both for their patients and their patient's families.

Smooth Transitions

Transitional care covers a range of services that need to occur whenever a patient moves from one treatment provider to another or from one level of care to another. By the way, these are the most vulnerable times in the healing process.

Examples of such transitions include:

- Inpatient to outpatient
- Hospitalization to home care
- Curative care to hospice
- Intensive care to a lower level of care, such as critical care or the general ward
- PCP to a specialist

Transitional care services ensure that these transitions happen smoothly and include the transfer of all required patient information. The exact services provided will vary according to the type of transition taking place.

In moving patients between specialists, the reason for the hand-off should be explained. A warm handoff can help patients feel more comfortable with the new treatment provider. Introducing a new provider by explaining their expertise can help establish a relationship of trust, especially if the person doing the introduction has a good relationship with the patient. When two providers are engaging in a joint meeting with a patient, they need to decide who will take the lead.

To envision the multifaceted nature of these services, let us revisit the types of transitional care provided by integrated residential addiction treatment centers. Early in their stay, patients will transition from the intense medical care provided by the onsite detox facility to the residential program. Communication between the primary doctor in the detox facility and the care coordinator in the residential program will ensure that the care coordinator is aware of the background and specific needs of the patients. Ideally, the same medical staff can provide the care throughout changes to levels of care.

When a physical move from one part of the center to another occurs, an orientation to the new setting may be necessary. Steps will also need to be taken to ease the patients' integration into the group that is ongoing in the residential program. In this transition, treatment modalities become more diverse, expressive, and cognitively focused.

When patients complete the residential program, another transition takes place. Patients can move from the inpatient program to a step-down unit or return home. Both involve a new situation where the patient can be exposed to additional stressors, some of which may have contributed to the substance use disorder in the first place.

Transitional services help the patients by connecting them with community resources—such as Alcoholics Anonymous and/or other mutual-aid support groups—to help them continue their recovery, and some centers put the outgoing patients in touch with alumni support in their area. With the patients' permission, their PCPs or BHPs will also be contacted with an update on their progress, so treatment and monitoring of the condition can continue during this level of care. All substance abuse treatment centers should help to transition patients to find housing, deal with transportation issues, assist with job placement, assist with legal needs, procure food services, and other practical matters that help them maintain recovery.

Smooth transitions of care are extremely important to a positive patient experience. So is effective patient engagement and an empowering approach that includes health literacy efforts. With all of these ingredients in place, you can ensure that the care you are providing is delivered via an excellent patient experience.

In other words, your audience may not be used to jazz. But improvisation does not have to be overwhelming, confusing, or disjointed. A good team of musicians can make sure that each person sitting out there in the darkness finds their groove.

References

Crowley, R. A., & Kirschner, N., for the Health and Public Policy Committee of the American College of Physicians. (2015). The integration of care for mental health, substance abuse, and other behavioral health conditions into primary care: Executive summary of an American College of Physicians position paper. *Annals of Internal Medicine, 163*, 298–299.

Eliacin, J. S. (2015). Factors influencing patients' preferences and perceived involvement in shared decision-making in mental health care. *Journal of Mental Health, 24*(1), 24–28.

Knight, D. K. (2014). Screening and assessment tools for measuring adolescent client needs and functioning in substance abuse treatment. *Substance Use & Misuse, 49*(7), 902–918.

Komaromy, M. M. (2018). Contingent engagement: What we learn from patients with complex health problems and low socioeconomic status. *Patient Education and Counseling, 101*(3), 524–531.

Poku, M. B. (2017). Patient relationship management: What the U.S. healthcare system can learn from other industries. *Journal of General Internal Medicine, 32*(1), 101–104.

Sharma, A. E. (2017). Engaging patients in primary care practice transformation: Theory, evidence and practice. *Family Practice, 33*(11), 1937–1944.

Zulman, D. M. (2018). Engaging high-need patients in intensive outpatient programs: A qualitative synthesis of engagement strategies. *Journal of General Internal Medicine, 33*(11), 1937–1944.

11 The Role of Leadership

Throughout my career, I have had the fortune of working as a member of multiple brilliant multidisciplinary care teams. In addition, I have treated hundreds of physicians for behavioral health (BH) issues and substance use disorders. Working primarily with professionals deepened my understanding of the complexity of behavior and addiction.

Here were men and women who worked in highly specialized fields. All of these people were accomplished and successful. They had excellent training, education, and skills. Yet they were all dealing with struggles that reduced them to being in the "survival mode" discussed earlier. They were suffering from unresolved trauma, complex mental health conditions, addiction, personality disorders, burnout, and workplace behavior that was threatening their careers. The main threat, however, was to the people who sought their care.

My time working in the professionals program at Pine Grove deepened my conviction that integrated therapy that addresses the convolution of addiction is the best form of treatment—and that it works best for the provider population in particular. Seeing and measuring the outcomes of those who had a long-term engagement, comprehensive treatment, vocational monitoring, and integration of values lead to a sense of achievement while reinforcing what I had learned at River Oaks. It was clear that the complexities of the psyche and the interplay of experiences and processes meant that treatment needed to be individualized. No single approach would be effective for everyone.

This has huge implications for healthcare leadership as well. I encourage leaders to adopt a style that reflects integrated care best practices. The role of the physician in integrated care is, first and foremost, to diagnose and treat illness—healthcare managers and executives play a similar role in the health of their organizations. Business leaders must ensure a high quality of care and drive business growth. They must identify barriers and dysfunctions and come up with a plan to resolve them. And, similar to an integrated care team's approach with a patient, the business leader's approach to any institutional disorder should be to act as early as possible and in a highly individualized way.

DOI: 10.4324/9781003128571-11

In alignment with the other four best practices of integrated care, the leadership should serve as the ultimate care manager to their employees. They should collect information through organizational assessments for the purpose of continuous improvement of their organization. They should model communication best practices in their own interactions. And they should actively engage in health promotion for providers and staff.

Other than the patients, the leadership of the organization has the biggest impact on the success or failure of integrated care.

Individualized Action

The vision and mission statement should be responsive to the needs of the individual, family, and community served while being updated when needed. Just like a treatment plan is for a patient.

And the integrated care transformation should be implemented as early as possible. Just like an intervention for a patient. So, let us talk about how to move forward.

The leadership has two primary responsibilities when seeking to move an organization to a collaborative care model. The first is committing long-term to the concept and necessary actions. Put most simply, when the leadership buys into the collaborative care model and actively promotes it, the model has the best chance of being adopted by the organization as a whole. Without leadership buy-in, the chances for success are much lower.

This commitment by the leadership needs to be longitudinal. For example, in surveying the success or failure of organizations that received a grant to implement integrated care, the Maine Health Access Foundation said, "If leadership changed, or leadership went on to other priorities, it compromised adoption and implementation of integrated approaches" (John Snow, Inc., 2014).

The second responsibility of leadership is to set the path that will allow the organization to make the vision a reality. This is a complex task, as moving to integrated care involves much more than simply implementing new policies and programs. Instead, it involves a wholesale reconceptualization of how healthcare is delivered. It is not an adjustment; it is a paradigm shift. As explained by Gina Lasky in an essay titled "Integrated Care: A Guide for Effective Implementation," "... genuine integration of behavioral health and primary care is complex and ultimately results in a significant change in organizational culture" (Laskey, 2017). Again it requires rethinking the entire organization from the ground up, a task that falls squarely on the shoulders of leadership.

A good place to start is core competencies. Your patients have a choice about where to seek care. What sets your institution apart? Across different categories of industries, organizations have articulated core competencies that govern employee performance and behavior. These core competencies should reflect the goals and values of the organization. Creating core competencies is an arduous process, but companies that have established and implemented them have noted positive effects between individual behavior and organizational success. Although core competency programs vary between organizations, researchers comparing these organizations have identified some common themes of adaptability, communication, and customer focus in successful ones.

Core competencies can be defined in multiple ways and at multiple levels of specificity. For example, the Substance Abuse and Mental Health Services Administration and the Health Resources and Services Administration (SAMHSA-HRSA) have nine core competencies for integrated care. These competencies are (1) interpersonal communication, (2) collaboration and teamwork, (3) screening and assessment, (4) care planning and care coordination, (5) intervention, (6) cultural competence and adaptation, (7) systems-oriented practice, (8) practice-based learning and quality improvement, and (9) informatics.

One group of researchers developed a comprehensive Competency Assessment Tool-Mental Health (CAT-MH) that defined 26 competencies rated by mental health professionals as important and suitable for additional education (Clasen, 2003). The CAT-MH included broader competencies (e.g., treating clients with dignity and respect and working as a team member), as well as more specific subject-matter competencies (e.g., knowing and applying the best therapies for different patient populations).

Core competencies can inform many aspects of an organization's activities—such as employee recruiting, performance evaluations, training, and promotions. Let us address recruiting first, as this is a key practice in building a staff that can provide integrated care. Carefully defining the specialties needed and then hiring people with the required expertise is part of the transition to integrated care, while an ongoing commitment to identifying and filling gaps in treatment knowledge allows the organization to continue the process of integration.

Several auxiliary tasks support the primary responsibilities and enable leaders to move their team toward the integration of behavioral and somatic healthcare. These include:

- Defining required expertise—The leadership is responsible for determining the skills and specialties that are needed for integrated care. These are not fixed models and talent can be sparse. The American College of Healthcare Executive's survey found that executive turnover rate held at 18% for the last three years with some states having as much as 38% turnover which limits tenor and longevity
- Staffing to fulfill mission and vision—Leaders need to ensure the organization has the proper team in place to become an integrated

health center. This involves both hiring and educating about the organization's mission. Team members should include not only medical/clinical professionals but also BH specialists, care managers, nurses, recovery coaches, case managers, discharge planners, transportation staff, laboratory staff, receptionists, and other support staff that contribute to the goal. And for multicultural populations being served, translators may need to be part of the team with whole team trainings on cultural competency and cultural humility (i.e., taking the position of seeking to understand and learn)
- Addressing staffing gaps and adjusting as needed—Ensuring proper staffing is not a one-time task. As people join and leave the organization and as needs change over time, leaders must continue to hire and train staff while redefining roles to meet new challenges
- Creating strong teams—The responsibility to create a strong team does not end when the staff has been hired. In fact, the process does not even begin until the staff is in place. A group of people working together does not necessarily constitute a team. It is up to the leadership to facilitate the creation of relationships and the sense of belonging that turn a bunch of individuals into a team. These four tasks, when performed properly, can contribute significantly to the realization of the leaders' vision of collaborative care

In Chapter 2, I talked about the history of integrated care as culminating in the development and evaluation of the PIP, a valuable tool for leaders implementing integrated care. Consider the following PIP items when recruiting and training personnel and developing core competencies for your practice.

Workflow Items:

1. We use a standard protocol to identify, assess, treat, and follow up with patients who need or can benefit from integrated BH
2. We use a registry to track identity and follow patients with diagnosed BH issues
3. We have BH clinicians who can see patients with serious mental illness and substance use disorders
4. We offer behavioral interventions for patients with chronic/complex medical illnesses
5. We offer complex or specialized BH therapies.
6. We offer evidence-based substance use interventions
7. We offer prescription medications for routine mental health and substance use diagnoses
8. We offer prescription medications for serious, complex, and co-occurring mental health and/or substance use diagnoses
9. We offer referral to non-clinical services outside of our practice

Workspace screening Items:

1. We screen eligible patients for at least one BH condition using a standardized procedure
2. We use practice-level data to screen for patients at risk for at least one complex or special need
3. Patients are screened at least annually for at least one behavioral condition related to a chronic medical problem
4. Patients are screened at least annually for lifestyle or behavioral risk factors
5. Screening data are presented to clinicians prior to (or at) patient encounters with recommendations for patient care

Patient Engagement

1. We successfully engage identified patients in behavioral care
2. We successfully retain patients in behavioral care
3. We have specific systems to identify and intervene on patients who did not initiate or maintain care
4. We have follow-up plans for all patients whose BH needs are resolved (Mullin, 2019)

These PIP items can help guide you in growing your team.

A number of factors and dynamics can affect a healthcare employer's ability to recruit, train, and retain capable staff. Developing the workforce begins with recruitment. Evidence-based strategies for hiring include combining monetary and non-monetary benefits and honestly representing the organization's culture and policies. The evidence also supports mixing formal recruiting strategies (e.g., such as campus fairs, advertising, and professional conferences) with informal strategies (e.g., such as networking and referrals). However, organizations should avoid over-reliance on informal recruitment or other strategies that may lead to a lack of diversity in the organization (Myers, 2007).

Implementing integrated care, in my experience, always involves a lot of recruitment. Doing it strategically is an investment in organizational outcomes. But it is not easy.

The leader must be prepared to be the "reviver" when realigning operations and culture with a new strategy like integrated care. A change management approach can transform an organization while stabilizing its members by offering confidence in the process and position within the industry. Really meta-leadership (i.e., self-awareness, self-understanding, and self-directed) is expected as partnering organizations will be positively influenced and guided by your adhering to ethical guidelines.

The Ultimate Care Managers

For decades, Robert Greenleaf served as an executive at AT&T where he discovered by traveling around the country to troubleshoot that the best companies had leadership that listened, was persuasive, accessed intuition and foresight, used language to communicate often, and pragmatic measured outcomes. In the 1970s, Greenleaf introduced the concept of servant leadership, which is published in essays and then a book in 1976. The concept of the desire to serve must first be achieved before consciously putting effort into a staff by focusing on their needs to be healthier, wiser, freer, more autonomous, and ultimately more likely themselves to become servants. This is a personal approach to removing barriers so that leaders can achieve.

We know that healthcare leadership is 70% people, 15% service, and 15% process. People need to be first and foremost, and leadership should be customized by knowing what the needs of the employees are so they develop. By focusing so much attention on people, power is shared within the organization. Therefore, leadership captures empowerment, communication, and accountability (Strategic Government Resources, n.d.). These concepts parallel the recovery process. They are life-affirming and life-restoring just like recovery. This leadership style goes beyond managing objectives and focuses on assisting with objections, obstacles, indifferences, roadblocks, and barriers.

The Assessment of the "Leader in Leadership" (Serpa , 2020) is a tool that my colleague, Roy Serpa, has used for years to invite leaders to answer honestly to determine potential areas of improvement. In this tool, participants ask themselves a series of questions:

1. What does leadership mean to you?
2. And as a leader, can you tell if something work-related is going wrong?
3. Does your team seek help from you?
4. As a leader, do you put your team's best interests ahead of your own?
5. As a leader, do you emphasize the importance of giving back to both the internal and external communities?
6. As a leader, do you give your team the freedom to handle difficult situations in the way that they feel best?

These questions can help you identify the gaps you need to fill in order to approach Robert Greenleaf's ideal. The servant leader is described as one who displays collaborative, ethical, and empathetic methods to serve others, rather than increasing their own power. A servant leader embodies characteristics (e.g., trust, foresight, awareness, stewardship, and commitment to the growth of people) that nurture an empowering working atmosphere. Your organization should have an emotional healing presence that shows sensitivity to others' personal concerns and the community at large. A productive work environment is one that makes employees feel valued.

These conceptual skills described above allow your leaders to be in a position to effectively support and assist others, especially direct reports. This encourages others to identify and solve problems, as well as determine when and how to complete tasks. This assistance to others allows for growth and improves the likelihood of success by demonstrating genuine concern for career paths. By putting subordinates first, servant leaders empower subordinates to face and resolve duties while interacting openly, fairly, and honestly at all times. Relationships allow leaders to know, understand, and support others with an emphasis on building long-term relationships with direct reports. Servant leadership means serving others first, even when self-sacrificing is required (Barbuto & Hayden, 2011; Spears, 2002).

There is a robust body of research discussing and analyzing the positive effects of adopting a servant leadership model in a variety of contexts. For example, in a U.S. study that surveyed 224 retailers, researchers found that servant leadership encouraged a favorable customer service climate (Hunter, 2013). They concluded that servant leadership led to positive behaviors from employees, such as helping coworkers and selling most products.

Moreover, the servant leadership model reduced turnover and disengagement. Similarly, an international study of 226 supervisor and supervisee units found that supervisees modeled their behavior on their supervisors (Arain, 2018). The research concluded both that servant leadership had a positive effect on the in-role performance of leadership skills from supervisees and that unethical or abusive behavior by supervisors was replicated by supervisees.

The positive impact of servant leadership was also noted in other cultures as researchers worked with groups in 187 hotels. They found that servant leadership improved work satisfaction, group dynamics, and employee professionalism (Linuesa-Langero, 2018).

The research regarding servant leadership specifically in the healthcare industry is less developed, although researchers have suggested that it would be a useful and productive paradigm to apply in that context as well.

In an article published in the Mayo Clinic Proceedings, researchers (Trastek, 2014) noted that the American healthcare system is "broken and unsustainable" and needs to be radically overhauled. They propose that the logical and cost-efficient solution would be for healthcare providers to adopt new models of leadership. After analyzing transactional, adaptive, and transformational models of leadership, the researchers concluded that servant leadership is the most appropriate leadership model for healthcare. Professional relationships between healthcare providers and provider-patient relationships would both benefit from adopting a servant leadership model, with the result of better outcomes and the use of resources for all participants.

In another study, researchers studied nurses and correlated areas that were of significant concern to their job satisfaction with characteristics of the servant leadership model. That study concluded that a servant leader model would be a beneficial style of supervision that could lead to greater professional development and satisfaction (Sturm, 2009).

Servant leadership is the management model best suited for leading an organization toward integrated care (Serpa, 2020). The servant-leader approach puts service first and simply states that the most important people in the organization are the staff. It defines a leader as someone who seeks to serve and is drawn to leadership as a way of serving. Such leaders promote change not through force but by example. They lead by embodying the type of culture they seek to instill and by empowering those in their organization to succeed. As Greenleaf (2002) put it:

> The difference manifests itself in the care taken by the servant—first to make sure that other people's highest priority needs are being served. The best test, and difficult to administer, is: Do those served grow as persons? Do they, while being served, become healthier, wiser, freer, more autonomous, more likely themselves to become servants? And, what is the effect on the least privileged in society? Will they benefit or at least not be further deprived? (p. 27)

Within the context of integrated care, servant-leaders enable their employees to transform the organization while allowing autonomy.

Information Collection and Continuous Improvement

Identifying team players with integrity, competence, good attitude, and passion is necessary but not sufficient. As a leader, you must also address gaps. You must identify individuals who are not the right fit for their respective position, recognize if a person is promoted but not capable of their job, monitor negative influences and those that are indifferent or noncommittal, and just average/below average staff.

Addressing these gaps is a challenge. But it is much easier when they can be brought to your attention through assessment, then monitored moving forward.

The power of self-assessment can never be underestimated either. As an organization, we require feedback and a stance of readiness when considering the implementation of integrated health (Substance Abuse & Mental Health Services Administration, 2009). This includes being able to answer key questions and complete key tasks, such as assigning the proper staff to deliver a readiness calculation:

1. Create a timeline and schedule for the self-assessment
2. Establish a responsible contact person within the organization
3. Establish a shared understanding of the assessment (i.e., including goals, objectives, and expectations) with the staff
4. Be transparent about what you are assessing
5. Understand what is the supervisory structure?
6. How does access to care occur?
7. Interview key stakeholders to gather varied perspectives about their experience:
    - Patients and families
    - Integrated treatment specialists
    - Medication prescribers (e.g., psychiatrists or nurses)
    - Therapists
    - Case managers
    - Rehabilitation services practitioners
    - Administrators
    - Employment specialists
    - Program leaders
8. Observe two full weeks of meetings, groups, and individual counseling sessions
9. Observe a treatment team and supervisory meeting
10. Conduct a chart review of at least ten charts to determine the level of integration
11. Find out how are you measuring your program's fidelity to evidence-based models?
12. How is client or patient data being collected?
13. How does your integrated program staff relate to your advisory group?
14. Identify organizational culture and biography along with the embedded values
15. Explore the weighted impact of key clinical and administrative leaders
16. What is the organization's professional identity?
17. Who is responsible for communicating this identity?

These responses and tasks can guide a transformation where feedback and change opportunities intersect to meet the complex needs of your patients.

The PIP is an incredibly valuable tool in organizational self-assessment. Implementing this model—and then continuously improving it based on data—offers credibility and quality metrics as uniformed scores can be representative of high standards of care. Leaders can use these scores to compare their organization to another. They can also use these scores to compare multiple sites in one system. It can be helpful to set a goal for all sites to achieve a minimum PIP score.

Fidelity is also an important goal. The success of any evidence-based mental health program depends in part on how faithfully the program is implemented (Ellickson, 2014). In the 1970s and 1980s, many programs to reintegrate individuals with severe mental illness led to disappointing results. This phenomenon prompted the identification of a need for formalized ways to assess program fidelity (Bond, 2011).

Fidelity scales are tools that have been developed to determine whether program failures are the result of how those programs were implemented or the design of the programs themselves (Paulson, 2002). Researchers have concluded that programs with higher program fidelity have better patient outcomes (Bond, 2011). All healthcare organizations should therefore assess the fidelity of their evidence-based programs in order to improve quality and to avoid program drift over time (Paulson, 2002).

In the 1990s, a group of researchers developed one of the earliest fidelity assessment models in the context of the Assertive Community Treatment (ACT) approach (Teague, 1998). The ACT approach is designed to help individuals with severe mental illnesses live harmoniously in their own communities and avoid hospitalization. However, ACT developers were unsure if new programs were following their model accurately. The researchers (Teague, 1998) designed the Dartmouth ACT Scale (DACTS). This assessment framework consists of 28 program criteria grouped into three categories: Human resources, organizational boundaries, and nature of services.

Other researchers have developed comparable fidelity assessment scales for different mental healthcare programs in different contexts. For example, researchers created a model of best practices for Crisis Resolution Teams (CRTs). With the goal of avoiding hospitalization, CRTs provide short-term, intensive in-home treatment to those in mental health crises (Lloyd-Evans, 2016). After the implementation of CRTs in the United Kingdom, however, hospitalizations had actually increased.

The problem prompted the researchers to create a fidelity assessment customized to this sector. Based on focus groups and interviews with CRT stakeholders, the researchers developed the CORE CRT Fidelity Scale. This 39-item tool defines the CRT model and provides means to assess and improve adherence to it. The researchers found that the CORE CRT Fidelity Scale was useful in identifying CRT providers who were less effective in complying with the models (Lloyd-Evans, 2016).

The DACTS is considered by many to be the gold standard for fidelity assessments, but the significant time and effort required to employ it on-site is a disadvantage (Rollins, 2017). One group of researchers comparing on-site fidelity assessments to phone-based or objective expert-scored fidelity assessments of VA mental health teams found that the latter were more cost-effective, although healthcare providers preferred the more laborious on-site assessments. Another study comparing on-site fidelity assessment with self-reported or over-the-phone fidelity assessment concluded that each method produced valid and reliable assessment results (McGrew, 2013).

Model Communication

Leaders have the responsibility to set the vision for integrated care. They must not only be committed to it personally. They have to communicate this vision to the rest of the organization.

There are clear practices that have been shown to be effective in facilitating integrated care. Throughout this book, I have referenced the rich communication insights offered by AHRQ's guidebook for integrated care. Leaders must take these communication practices to heart and use them in their own interactions with patients and staff.

Leaders have many opportunities to model good communication because leadership responsibilities include many necessary communication tasks. Examples include valuing everyone's time and maintaining responsibility for the management of meetings, all-staff meetings, town hall meetings, communication blast calls to all employees with key updates via phone, annual reward and recognition of exceptional employees, and focus groups when developing new service lines/projects.

In AHRQ's research to develop their guidebook for integrated care, the agency found that integrated care was facilitated by a clearly articulated mission and vision that advocated integrated care. Leaders define their vision for care and communicate this to the staff. When the staff is able to articulate the vision and is aware of buy-in by the organization's leadership, integrated care is easier to achieve.

Communication between leaders and staff is important. According to a large body of research, the supervisor-employee relationship has a significant influence on employee retention and even the quality of patient care.

One study found that a positive relationship can lead employees to overlook other problematic aspects of a job or organization. Factors that contribute to a deteriorating relationship with a supervisor include lack of feedback or recognition and inadequate training. These researchers suggest that retaining employees begins with the supervisor's effort to develop sincere work relationships (Wallach, 2012).

Another study of millennial employees supports that suggestion. The researchers concluded that adequate and continuing communication between management and employees was strongly related to the employee's job engagement and commitment (Walden, 2017). Communication should cover individual issues such as job performance and organization-wide issues. This will enhance feelings of security and entrust in the goodness of humanity. This allows one to continuously maintain a positive alignment with others and to refute a negative world view. This holding and secure base is similar to attachment theory in psychotherapy.

One study in the healthcare context recognized that employee loyalty is critical because staff turnover is costly, inefficient, and can compromise patient care. Researchers advise that health organizations should adopt a marketing-driven approach to staffing, more specifically the relationship marketing approach to maintaining physician loyalty (Peltier, 1997). In general, relationship marketing is based on the idea that it is less expensive eventually to maintain the same customers rather than replacing them with new customers. Relationship marketing operates on three levels, and relationships are strongest when all three are established: Financial bonds, social bonds, and structural bonds (Peltier, 1997).

In the healthcare context, the level of financial bonds would take the form of financial incentives to retain physicians or employees. However, this is the weakest level of bond because other organizations can always offer more money. Social bonds encompass practices such as open communication between management and physicians, as well as developing an environment in which physicians can voice their concerns, have them addressed, and receive additional support. The strongest level of bond is structural bonds, which develop when physicians have a role in deciding how medical services are delivered. To develop these bonds, the relationship between physician and organization needs trust, mutual commitment, effective communication, and individualized relationships.

One rural clinic employed 68 physicians in a town of 50,000. The clinic implemented a relationship-marketing strategy for physician retention. The program utilized information-gathering techniques including interviews, questionnaires, and focus groups to collect data about improving physician morale. Based on that input, the clinic not only addressed specific concerns and complaints but also focused on creating a relationship-building framework. Researchers found that the program improved physician satisfaction by continuing the process of listening to their concerns. The relationship-building approach proved to be very successful. No physicians left the clinic in the three following years (Peltier, 1997).

This confirms the significance of organizational and supervisor support in the degree that employees feel valued. One group conducted a survey of 35 nurses, therapists, technicians, and physicians. The findings revealed that their employers expressed their value through words of affirmation (e.g., positive feedback in performance reviews), tangible gifts (e.g., food and gift cards), acts of service (e.g., assisting during heavy workloads), and quality time (e.g., being available to process stressful work incidents immediately after they happened). The researchers concluded that healthcare workers who feel cared for by their employers are better equipped to care for their patients (Baggett, 2016).

Health Promotion

We have already established that integrated care is good for providers. This team-based model of care offers providers support in performing the job, opens up opportunities for early intervention in providers' own mental health, and increases job satisfaction. Furthermore, this patient-centered process should lead to lower levels of stress among care providers and higher levels of efficiency despite increasing the complexity of care (Substance Abuse and Mental Health Services Administration).

But leaders still face the responsibility of going further to support the health of their providers and other staff. A big part of that is taking active steps to address burnout.

There is a developing body of research regarding the effectiveness of programs specifically designed to target burnout and improve employee wellness and retention. In one study, researchers examined a burnout intervention program consisting of weekly meetings of six to eight mental health workers. The meetings were conducted by a psychologist. In the meetings, participants discussed the work environment, career goals and expectations, self-image, and action plans. One year after the program, they found positive outcomes, including measurable decreases in emotional exhaustion and the length of absences from work. They noted that, although individual interventions can be successful, organization-wide approaches could be more effective.

That suggestion finds support in the work by another group of researchers who reviewed three categories of burnout-prevention programs in the healthcare context: (1) Person-directed interventions such as cognitive behavioral training, adaptive skills training, and social support; (2) organization-directed interventions such as adjustments to work process and schedules, as well as work performance appraisals; and (3) programs that combined both types of interventions. They concluded that programs combining both person-directed and organization-directed interventions had the most significant and long-lasting effects on reducing burnout.

There are several commonly used burnout measurement tools. In addition to the Maslach Burnout Inventory, there are the Staff Burnout Scale for Health Professionals and the Burnout Measure. The former includes a 30-item questionnaire utilizing a 6-point Likert scale, and the latter consists of a 21-item questionnaire utilizing a 7-point Likert scale. These tools can be utilized to understand individual's, group's, and departmental needs and should be conducted regularly by collegial and external supervisors. This will impact individuals while resulting in appropriate therapeutic interventions which result in lower levels of remission.

After evaluating the presence of burnout in your organization, the first step for leadership can be as simple as acknowledging burnout and encouraging employees to think about their self-care. Health care organizations can also combat burnout by emphasizing the importance of self-care and mental health. This can be accomplished by providing personal coverage that explicitly allows physicians to take time off work to attend therapeutic appointments, and providing mindfulness or exercise programs and gym memberships. Stanford and Mount Sinai hospitals, for example, took a much more intensive approach by hiring chief wellness officers to serve on their administrative team.

The Mayo Clinic has outlined strategies to combat burnout in the healthcare profession. These strategies are to (1) involve leadership, (2) choose incentives wisely, (3) encourage work–life balance, (4) encourage peer support, (5) furnish resources for self-care and mental health, and (6) target burnout from day one of medical school (Reith, 2018). The Mayo Clinic advises organizations to consider other incentives, such as schedule flexibility or time off work, instead of financial incentives because productivity-based compensation can itself lead to burnout. In a study of long-term care facilities in Hawaii, researchers noted that burnout decreased where employees had increased social support from supervisors and the organization, control over their schedule, and job satisfaction (Kim, 2019).

The Mayo Clinic also stresses the importance of interactions between physicians to decrease burnout—this is a challenge because physicians are often bogged down with documentation and cannot interact with each other. To encourage interactions between physicians and other professionals, healthcare organizations can provide free coffee and snacks at certain gathering spots.

Employers can attempt to address burnout before it occurs through resiliency training programs. Resiliency "is the ability to manage and grow throughout life's challenges." Researchers studied healthcare employees who participated in a 12-week resiliency program conducted by physicians and certified wellness coaches that addressed topics including stress, compassion, meditation, and relevant skill-building. The research found after the training that employees reported improvements in stress, quality of life, and health behaviors (Werneburg, 2018).

Wellness programs should also target somatic health. It is well-documented that Americans and healthcare providers are among those who live unhealthy lifestyles. If current health trends do not change, health experts predict a sharp increase in serious health problems and early deaths from preventable diseases in the coming years (Hall, 2008). Manageable diseases such as diabetes and heart disease are largely to blame for skyrocketing healthcare costs (Isehunwa, 2017). Businesses are bearing the brunt of rising healthcare costs; as many as 41.7% of employers blame the cost of healthcare as the biggest challenge to their bottom line (Kumar, 2009). Employee wellness programs are one approach businesses are implementing to battle healthcare costs. Using the workplace as a venue for modifying behavior makes sense because Americans spend much of their time at work (Emerson, 2017).

The purpose of employee wellness programs is to incentivize employees to adopt healthier behaviors. Employers who launch employee wellness programs typically offer health screens, seminars, health-related fairs, on-site gyms, and/or healthier food options in vending machines. For example, one midwestern manufacturing program implemented an employee pedometer program and installed wellness kiosks equipped with biometric scans. The researchers studied the results of the pedometer program and found that the employee wellness program was a success. The company reported a decrease in work-related injuries, improved biometric pressure, and overall healthier worker lifestyles in the first year (Swayze, 2013).

A study of an employee wellness program at the University of California, Los Angeles (UCLA) focused on a three-month exercise and nutrition program within the workplace wellness program. They found significant improvements in employee physical health, mental health, stress, energy level, social satisfaction, self-efficacy, and quality of life (Emerson, 2017).

Although employee wellness programs benefit employees, employers also have strong financial motivations to implement such programs. Researchers analyzed three years' worth of data from a wellness program at an American financial institution and found improvements in employee performance ratings, job satisfaction, intention to stay, and turnover (Ott-Holland, 2019). Another study of an American company found a link between healthier eating habits, physical condition, and productivity (Kumar, 2009). Wellness programs may also encourage employees to make other beneficial health decisions, such as utilizing more preventive healthcare treatments, such as flu vaccines and blood pressure, diabetes, and cholesterol tests, which may also reduce long-term healthcare costs (Isehunwa, 2017).

Once an employer has hired the workforce it wants, it must work actively to retain them. Although integrated care is itself a way to boost job satisfaction, leaders can do more. Employee satisfaction in healthcare settings strongly correlates to both employee retention and patient satisfaction (Collins, 2008).

Studies indicate that programs emphasizing workplace fun—such as casual dress days, recognition programs, and complimentary snacks—contribute to employee satisfaction. Researchers also find that feeling disconnected from work is a primary driver of employee turnover. To avoid employee loss, managers should prioritize mentoring and ongoing training.

The Virginia Commonwealth University (VCU) Medical Center lost six social workers in one department in one year, prompting researchers to analyze social worker retention and professional development. The VCU Medical Center formed a retention committee to examine the hospital's problem. The committee identified pay, communication with management, and advancement opportunities as the primary issues with employee retention. The committee recommended concrete steps, such as pay raises, a clinical ladder system for advancement, and improved two-way communication channels between employees and management. After implementing those steps, the department lost only one employee the following year (Blosser, 2010).

In a national survey, direct care workers were asked the single most important thing their employer could do to improve their job; the most common answers were higher pay, better communication, and supervision, and being appreciated, listened to, and treated with respect (Kemper, 2008). Other research confirms that organizational and supervisor support is critical to maintaining a positive environment for healthcare workers. In another study, data gathered from nurses in Illinois and North Carolina and concluded that nurses who plan to leave their current job reported feeling less autonomy and support from their peers (Yoon, 2016).

As a culture of wellness spreads throughout your organization, a full self-assessment is required. This evaluation must be organization-wide with a critical eye on wellness provided by the organization. Wellness may encompass benefits, community activities and connections, rewards and recognition by leadership, workforce development, good self-management language utilized by all staff (i.e., positive exchanges), organizational policies, and performance evaluation with clear competencies/expectations. Once this appraisal is complete, a simple three-question evaluation can guide your readiness:

1. What should you keep doing?
2. What should you stop doing?
3. And what should you start doing?

Conclusion

The leader must possess the ability to be both a transactional leader (i.e., day-to-day management) and a transformational leader (i.e., investigates the future and defines the direction for the organization) (Threnhauser, 2019). Implementing integrated care with a servant-leadership approach goes a long way to reaching transformational goals.

This leads to an atmosphere of accountability and ownership, empowering the staff to be a part of the direction of the organization. It increases job satisfaction, and confidence in patient care, patient and family treatment experience, and profitability.

At the front end of an implementation of integrated care, the effort is great, and all change is driven by intention and action. But as an organization gets further along, it begins to develop organic movement toward the goal of integrated care. As more exposure occurs, a sense of mastery, confidence, and competencies builds, which is the cornerstone of healing collectively (Raney, 2017).

References

Arain, G. (2018). The impact of leadership style on moral identity and subsequent in-role performance: A moderated mediation analysis. *Ethics & Behavior, 28*(8), 613–627.

Baggett, M. G. (2016). Exploring the human emotion of feeling cared for in the workplace. *Journal of Nursing Management, 24*(6), 816–824.

Barbuto, J., & Hayden, R. W. (2011). Testing relationships between servant leadership dimensions and Leader Member Exchange (LMX). *Journal of Leadership Education, 10*(2), 22–37.

Blosser, J. C. (2010). Factors that influence retention and professional development in social workers. *Administration in Social Work, 34*(2), 168–177.

Bond, G. R. (2011). Measurement of fidelity of implementation of evidence-based practices: Case example of the IPS Fidelity Scale. *Clinical Psychology: Science & Practice, 18*(2), 126–141.

Clasen, C. M. (2003). Development of the competency assessment tool-mental health: An instrument to assess core competencies for mental health care workers. *Psychiatric Rehabilitation Journal, 27*(1), 10–17.

Collins, K. C. (2008). Employee satisfaction and employee retention: Catalysts to patient satisfaction. *The Health Care Manager, 27*(3), 245–251.

Ellickson, P. L. (2014). You've shown the program model is effective. Now what? *New Directions for Youth Development, 141*, 95–105.

Emerson, N. D. (2017). Effects of an employee exercise programme on mental health. *Occupational Medicine, 67*(2), 128–134.

Greenleaf, R. K. (2002). *Servant leadership: A journey into the nature of legitimate power and greatness*, 25th anniversary ed. New York, NY: Paulist Press.

Hall, B. (2008). Health incentives: The science and art of motivating health behaviors. *Benefits Quarterly, 24*(2), 12–22.

Hunter, E. N. (2013). Servant leaders inspire servant followers: Antecedents and outcomes for employees and the organization. *Leadership Quarterly, 24*(2), 316–331.

Isehunwa, O. O. (2017). Access to employee wellness programs and use of preventive care services among U.S. adults. *American Journal of Preventive Medicine, 53*(6), 854–865.

John Snow, Inc. (2014). *Final evaluation report*. Maine Health Access Foundation. Retrieved from https://www.jsi.com/JSIInternet/Inc/Common/_download_pub.cfm?id=16215&lid=3

Kemper, P. H.-K. (2008). What do direct care workers say about improve their jobs? Differences across settings. *Gerontologist, 48*, 17–25.

Kim, B., Liu, L., Ishikawa, H., and Park, S. H. (2019). Relationships between social support, job autonomy, job satisfaction, and burnout among care workers in long-term care facilities in Hawaii. *Educational Gerontology, 45*(1), 57–68, DOI: 10.1080/03601277.2019.1580938

Kumar, S. M. (2009). Operation impact of employee wellness programs: A business case study. *International Journal of Productivity and Performance Management, 58*(6), 581–597.

Laskey, G. B. (2017). Organizational leadership and cultural change. In L. E. Raney, *Integrated care: A guide for effective implementation* (p. 42). Arlington, VA: American Psychiatric Association.

Linuesa-Langero, J. R. P. H. (2018). Integrating servant leadership into managerial strategy to build group social capital: The mediating role of group citizenship behavior. *Journal of Business Ethics, 152*(4), 899–916.

Lloyd-Evans, B. B. (2016). Development of a measure of model fidelity for mental health Crisis Resolution Teams. *BMC Psychiatry, 16*, 1–12.

McGrew, J. H. B. (2013). A comparison of self-reported and phone-administered methods of ACT fidelity assessment: A pilot study in Indiana. *Psychiatric Services, 64*(3), 272–276.

Mullin, D. H. (2019). Measuring the integration of primary care and behavioral health services. *Health Services Research, 54*(2), 379–389.

Myers, V. L. (2007). Recruitment and retention of a diverse workforce: Challenges and opportunities. *Journal of Healthcare Management, 52*(5), 290–298.

Ott-Holland, C. J. (2019). Examining wellness programs over time: Predicting participation and workplace outcomes. *Journal of Occupational Health Psychology, 24*(1), 163–179.

Paulson, R. I. (2002). Beyond components: Using fidelity scales to measure and assure choice in program implementation and quality assurance. *Community Mental Health Journal, 38*(2), 119–128.

Peltier, J. W. (1997). Building relationships with physicians. *Marketing Health Services, 17*(3), 12–18.

Raney, L. E. (2017). *Integrated care: A guide for effective implementation*. Washington, DC: American Psychiatric Association Publishing.

Reith, T. P. (2018). Burnout in United States healthcare professionals: A narrative review. *Cureus, 10*(12), p.e3681-e3681.

Rollins, A. K. (2017). Comparing the costs and acceptability of three fidelity assessment methods for assertive community treatment. *Administration & Policy in Mental Health & Mental Health Services Research, 44*, 810–816.

Serpa, R. (2020, December). Personal communication.

Spears, L. C. (2002). *Focus on leadership: Servant-leadership for the twenty-first century*. New York: John Wiley & Sons, Inc.

Strategic Government Resources. (n.d.). *Assessments*. Retrieved from Strategic Government Resources: https://www.governmentresource.com/leadership-development/assessments

Sturm, B. A. (2009). Principles of servant-leadership in community health nursing. *Home Health Management & Practice, 21*(2), 82–89.

Substance Abuse and Mental Health Services Administration. (2009). In C. F. Services (Ed.), *Integrated treatment for co-occurring disorders: Evaluating your program*. Rockville, MD: US Department of Health and Human Services.

Substance Abuse and Mental Health Services Administration. (n.d.). *A quick start guide to behavioral health integration for safety-net primary care providers*. Retrieved from SAMHSA-HRSA Center for Integrated Health Solutions (CIHS): https://www.samhsa.gov/integrated-health-solutions

Swayze, J. S. (2013). Employee wellness program outcomes: A case study. *Journal of Workplace Behavioral Health, 28*(1), 46–61.

Teague, G. B. (1998). Dartmouth ACT scale. *American Journal of Orthopsychiatry, 68*, 216–232.

Threnhauser, S. C. (2019, May 23). *Open minds*. Retrieved from https://openminds.com/market-intelligence/executive-briefings/leadership-the-other-talent-shortage/

Trastek, V. F., Hamilton, N. W., and Niles, E. E. (2014). Leadership models in health care—A case for servant leadership. *Mayo Clinic Proceedings, 89*(3), 374–381. https://doi.org/10.1016/j.mayocp.2013.10.012

Walden, J. J. (2017). Employee communication, job engagement, and organizational commitment: A study of members of the Millennial Generation. *Journal of Public Relations Research, 29*(2–3), 73–89.

Mackenzie, Maureen L. Ph.D. and Wallach, Darren F. MBA (2012). The Boss-Employee Relationship: Influence on Job Retention. *Faculty Works: Business*, 11, https://digitalcommons.molloy.edu/bus_fac/11

Werneburg, B. L. (2018). Improving resiliency in healthcare employees. *American Journal of Health Behavior, 42*(1), 39–50.

Yoon, S. P. (2016). Factors affecting job satisfaction among agency-employed home health aides. *Home Health Care Management & Practice, 28*(1), 57–69.

12 Coordinated Care on a Spectrum

Implementing integrated care can seem a daunting task given the amount of integration involved. Fortunately, integrated care is not an all-or-nothing proposition.

This chapter explains how the Substance Abuse and Mental Health Services Administration defines six levels of integration to help providers gauge their progress. These run from Level 1 (minimal collaboration) to Level 6 (close collaboration in a fully integrated system). This chapter also provides examples of integrated care, including patient-centered health homes and trans-organizational cooperation, along with ways to move from one level of integration to the next.

Chapter 2 referenced National Survey of Accountable Care Organizations data that found few ACOs having nearly complete or fully complete integration of behavioral health and primary care, while almost half reported no integration at all. Those reporting more integration were typically larger healthcare systems with behavioral health provider groups internally. Three models have been identified as: (1) a consulting model or consultative service, (2) a co-location model where space is shared between primary care and behavioral health providers, and (3) the embedded model in which behavioral health providers work directly in primary care teams

In an ideal world, mental and somatic healthcare would be fully integrated, with collaboration taking place in one facility among various practitioners who are involved in developing a single treatment plan to address the needs of each individual patient. Increased access to care and increased health literacy are both facilitated by the co-location of behavioral health and primary care services when possible. The reality, however, is that many practices are not integrated as stated above, and even practices that are trying to implement full integration take time and effort to achieve it. Most practices fall somewhere in between.

Recognizing this, the US government's Substance Abuse and Mental Health Services Administration has devised a scale that allows organizations to assess their level of integration. This not only provides them with an idea of where they currently are but also gives them an idea of how to move forward, providing a road map to achieving full integration.

DOI: 10.4324/9781003128571-12

Although this scale can be very helpful, I also find fault with key aspects of it, as I will explain.

This is divided into six levels that fall into three groups (Heath, 2013):

- Coordinated Care (Levels 1–2)
- Co-located Care (Levels 3–4)
- Integrated Care (Levels 5–6)

For each level, SAMHSA's framework indicates how care providers work and how the patient experiences treatment.

Level 1 is characterized by minimal collaboration. Mental and physical healthcare providers work in different facilities and only rarely consult with one another. Each provider develops a treatment plan in isolation from the other. Behavioral and somatic issues are addressed as separate problems. The patient is left navigating two different systems, essentially in isolation.

Level 2 involves basic collaboration, though providers are still at different sites or co-located. Their communication is driven by patient needs, so collaboration is on an ad hoc basis. At this level, each provider generally has an appreciation for the contributions of those in other fields. Separate treatment plans are still maintained, although some sharing of patient information may be done through health information exchanges. The patient still sees practitioners at multiple sites but will sometimes do so because of a referral from one of the providers.

Although Levels 1 and 2 fall into the category of Coordinated Care, I should say that I personally do not think Levels 1–2 qualify as "coordinated" at all. At this point, there is still no system interoperability or shared platforms, treatment plans are completely siloed, and screenings are not standardized. Coordinated Care, in my view, is a misnomer.

Co-located care begins at Level 3, which continues the basic collaboration of Level 2 but, SAMHSA delineates these levels as having providers work out of a shared facility. Systems remain separate, but mental and physical care providers will consult regularly, though usually not in person. Providers may use an agreed set of screenings to assess patient health. Patient needs are addressed separately but in the same location, removing one barrier to treatment.

I think the continuum should be revised to consider integration independent of co-location. Those of us who implement integrated careers as our careers have much more experience in building up large systems—recruiting staff, adding facilities, etc. So, we naturally biased (and have more evidence for) the model where multiple disciplines collaborate within the same organization. And I do believe that is the optimal model. I also believe, however, that it is possible for healthcare providers to achieve the highest level of integration without sharing the same building or even the same employer. It would not be easy though. It would require excellent communication, EHR interoperability, and the ability to expand one's philosophy of care.

With Level 4, collaboration is improved, with regular in-person consultations on some patients and unified treatment plans sometimes being developed. Information is shared more frequently, and they share some systems for patient scheduling and health information. A practice-wide set of screenings is used. Patient needs are still treated separately, but warm hand-offs may occur between specialties. Patients may still perceive mental and physical healthcare as separate services. Level 4 is the first one that I would consider to be truly coordinated.

Even within integrated care (Levels 5–6), distinctions can be made in the amount of integration. At Level 5, care is co-located and practitioners collaborate closely. In-person consultations are frequent, and both behavioral and somatic specialists have an in-depth understanding of the role the others play in the system. The practice begins to resemble a unified organization. Patients will experience it as a single entity, and providers see themselves as a team. They likely use a single system for billing and record-keeping.

Level 6 indicates full collaboration. The team operates in a single facility where an integrated system is used for scheduling, billing, and medical information across the board. Communication is frequent at all levels, and collaboration is driven by a shared concept of team care. A standardized set of behavioral and somatic screenings, tailored to individual patient populations, are administered by all providers. Patients are treated under a single treatment plan developed and monitored by team members from all disciplines. Patients experience the practice as a unified whole and seamlessly receive care for all aspects of their mental and physical health issues.

These services must be provided within the context of whole-person care so the philosophy is clearly communicated between practitioners and within organizations. If multiple services are provided but not communicated, then integrated care is not being practiced. Organizations can start with minor changes which transfer them down the continuum by setting up systems, policies, and processes that adhere to this framework. Consider redesigning your assessment.

Screenings are an important tool for diagnosing illnesses outside of one's specialty. At Level 2, screenings normally remain independent, with PCPs and BHPs deciding which screens to use on their own. As care moves into Levels 3–4, screens may begin to be selected through a collaborative process. PCPs can inform BHPs about which screens should be used with which patient populations. BHPs can, in turn, advise PCPs about screening tools for various mental health issues, including the detection of a substance use disorder. Each can also educate the other about how to interpret the scores from particular assessment tools and the next steps that should be taken to determine the patient's treatment needs.

Patient-Centered Medical Homes

Although trans-organizational cooperation can help organizations improve the level of healthcare they provide, moving into Levels 5 and 6 generally requires greater integration and coordination between PCPs and BHPs that comes from working at the same site. At the level of highest integration, the patient-centered medical home (PCMH) becomes the model for providing care.

PCMH is a collection of practices providing a range of services that meet all the physical and mental healthcare needs of patients. The model promotes comprehensive care management, care coordination, health promotion, comprehensive transitional care, individual and family support, and referral to community and social support. The services have provisions of care, policy and procedure manuals, relevant training sources, and agility when considering health disparities.

The US Department of Health and Human Services' Agency for Healthcare Research and Quality (AHRQ) espouses the development of PCMHs (Agency for Healthcare Research and Quality, n.d.):

> "The Agency for Healthcare Research and Quality recognizes that revitalizing the Nation's primary care system is foundational to achieving high-quality, accessible, efficient health care for all Americans. The patient-centered medical home ... is a promising model for transforming the organization and delivery of primary care."

AHRQ also provides an overview of PCMHs, tools for implementation, and research concerning evidence-based practices and program evaluation (Mauer, Behavioral health/primary care integration and the person-centered healthcare home, 2009).

Ideally, all patient care services would be collocated, as SAMHSA describes in its top two levels of care integration. But although standard behavioral and somatic health services need to be collocated, it is obviously not practical for every PCMH to have every single specialist imaginable working at the same location.

Despite its name, a PCMH is not a location. These are not necessarily home health services. Consider the "home" model of care a metaphor, not a reference to the facility. Some specialists will be located in other practices. But the close collaboration of these specialists and integration of the care they provide make them part of the home.

In 2007, the American Academy of Family Physicians, the American Academy of Pediatrics, the American College of Physicians, and the American Osteopathic Association published their "Joint Principles of the Patient-Centered Medical Home" (American Academy of Family Physicians (AAFP), American Academy of Pediatrics (AAP), American

College of Physicians (ACP), American Osteopathic Association (AOA), 2007). It laid out the following characteristic of a PCMH:

- Each patient has an ongoing relationship with a personal physician trained to provide first contact, continuous, and comprehensive care
- The personal physician leads a team of individuals at the practice level who collectively take responsibility for the ongoing care of patients
- Care is oriented to the whole person, providing care for all stages of life, including acute care, chronic care, preventive services, and end-of-life care
- Care is coordinated and/or integrated across all elements of the complex healthcare system
- Care system and the patient's community. Care is facilitated by documentation, information technology, health information exchange, and other means to assure that patients get the indicated care when and where they need and want it in a culturally and linguistically appropriate manner
- Quality and safety are maintained through the use of evidence-based practices
- Enhanced access to care is available through systems such as open scheduling, expanded hours, and new options for communication between patients, their personal physician, and practice staff
- Payment appropriately recognizes the added value provided to patients

Other organizations have outlined similar sets of characteristics. In discussing the integration of behavioral health into PCMHs, this chapter will focus on six core services critical to such integrated care: Comprehensive care management, care coordination, health promotion, comprehensive transitional care, individual and family support, and referral to community and social support services.

An important aspect of integrated care is the management of the care process. The PCMH is a model of care delivery that generally puts a case manager, generally a PCP, in charge of directing a patient's overall course of care. The case manager is in charge of determining the overall course of a patient's treatment for individual issues and for making sure that all facets of a patient's health are treated in a timely manner and in the appropriate order. The goal is to engage in practices that promote health, thereby heading off acute problems before they develop. Within a PCMH, treatment plans are developed by a team that includes both somatic and behavioral health specialists.

Such an approach not only leads to a better quality of life but also controls healthcare costs. The need to assess and provide solid health indicators with regards to obesity, smoking, sleep, medication adherence, and self-management of chronic conditions. Comprehensive Transitional Care requires attention at all interims as these are the most vulnerable times for those with mental health needs. The ability to have security and confidence in care providers reduces one's stress when recovering and healing as the need to repeat information and timelines is eliminated. Families' support or orientation to becoming a key member of the care team is often neglected in siloed systems. The family members are usually taxed with understanding medical terminology, coordinating services, and managing their own stress. The need to draw upon community resources has always been crucial, but critically important in today's market. We have shifted from an expert referral system to a consumer-driven system where family members are left to seek the necessary services while usually being ill prepared for this responsibility. This referral process and social support needs to be an investment in the integrated model.

The hallmark of a PCMH is its provision of care that covers all aspects of a patient's physical and mental health. Services for all stages of life are available, making it a one-stop shop for addiction and behavioral health.

Four Quadrant Clinical Integration Model

If your organization specializes in serving a niche population, your PCMH may not need to provide every service throughout the full continuum of care. The Four Quadrant Clinical Integration Model is a helpful tool in determining which services need to be provided by a PCMH. The National Association of State Mental Health Program Directors and the National Association of State Alcohol and Drug Abuse Directors initially developed the model in 1998. It was updated and expanded by the National Council for Community Behavioral Healthcare in 2009 and 2010 (Mauer, 2009). The model describes the particular services that are required in a PCMH to serve specific patient populations.

The Four Quadrant Model plots patient populations along two axes. One axis represents their level of physical health problems. The other indicates their risk for behavioral health issues and substance use disorders. This results in four quadrants:

- Quadrant I: Low risk/complexity for both behavioral and physical health problems
- Quadrant II: High risk/complexity for behavioral issues and low risk/complexity for physical health problems
- Quadrant III: Low risk/complexity for behavioral issues and high risk/complexity for physical health problems
- Quadrant IV: High risk/complexity for both behavioral and physical health problems

The quadrants are used for indicating services used by particular patient populations. They are not intended to indicate where individuals should receive treatment (Mauer, 2010). In general, primary practices will serve patients in Quadrants I and III, while behavioral health providers treat patient populations that fall into Quadrants II and IV. The process of transitions to higher or lower levels of care or stepped care, which refers to providing the patient with the appropriate level of care, should be developed to provide people with the appropriate levels of care.

Quadrant I covers patients with low to moderate risk and complexity in both physical and behavioral health. A population in this quadrant is best served in a primary care setting that incorporates several aspects of behavioral healthcare, including screening for behavioral health and substance use. Patients who present with more complex behavioral problems or fully developed substance use disorders and patients who are not responding to treatment can be referred to a behavioral health facility.

Patients in Quadrant III are those with more complex somatic health problems who remain at low risk for behavioral health problems. The primary care setting remains the best location for treatment. All elements of care in Quadrant I are still in place, but the participation of medical specialists for the treatment of more serious problems is required. Because of the greater frequency of behavioral health problems among people with chronic physical health problems, the BHP should be included in the treatment process to catch signs of developing mental health issues.

Care for patients in Quadrants II and IV is best located in behavioral health settings. Patients in Quadrant II have a high risk/complexity of behavioral health issues but have overall good physical health (Mauer, 2010). Along with the standard practitioners on the mental health side, a center that serves patients in this quadrant needs to either have a PCP employed full-time or a nurse practitioner who is supervised by an off-site PCP. Standard health screenings and wellness programs should be a part of the services. As in Quadrant IV, these patients face an increased risk of having multiple conditions—both physical and mental. So, a heightened sensitivity to signs of developing problems is required.

Quadrant IV comprises patient populations at high risk/complexity of both somatic and behavioral health issues. All services available in Quadrant II need to be available for these patients, along with enhanced care to deal with the increased physical problems. For patients with substance use disorders, proper care will require an addiction treatment center. Chronic care management needs to be implemented, and self-management should be taught to empower patients to take control of their conditions. The addition of lower and higher levels of care allows the practice to respond at appropriate levels depending on the severity of the condition. The PCP or NP will need to have a relationship with a number of specialists for consultation and referral for specific medical needs.

References

Agency for Healthcare Research and Quality. (n.d.). *Patient-centered medical home resource center*. Retrieved from Agency for Healthcare Research and Quality: https://www.pcmh.ahrq.gov/

American Academy of Family Physicians (AAFP), American Academy of Pediatrics (AAP), American College of Physicians (ACP), American Osteopathic Association (AOA). (2007, March). *Joint principles of the patient-centered medical home*. Retrieved from American Academy of Family Physicians (AAFP): https://www.aafp.org/dam/AAFP/documents/practice_management/pcmh/initiatives/PCMHJoint.pdf

Mauer, B. J. (2009). *Behavioral health/primary care integration and the person centered healthcare home*. Washington, DC: National Council for Behavioral Health.

Mauer, B. J. (2010). *Substance use disorders and the person-centered healthcare home*. Washington, DC: National Council for Behavioral Health.

13 Considerations for Different Settings

Integrating mental and somatic care improves the level of mental healthcare that takes place in primary care settings, and it reaches the people who are most likely to need treatment for mental health issues. In a behavioral health setting, it provides physical healthcare to a population that is often unable to receive adequate somatic care but needs it the most.

So how does integrated care look in both mental and physical care settings? This chapter will discuss various models of integration and detail what each one looks like in practice.

Bringing Behavioral Care into Primary Care Settings

Consider Transcranial Magnetic Stimulation (TMS) which is an FDA-approved non-invasive alternative to antidepressants or other treatments for depression. It has been proven safe and effective when compared to other neurostimulation techniques such as deep brain stimulation (DBS), ECT, and epidural cortical stimulation for treating psychiatric disorders, addictions, neurological disorders, chronic pain, and behavioral disorders. First demonstrated in 1985 by Magstim, TMS uses electromagnetic induction to influence nearby cells to fire and synchronize. It is painless and at the same time can produce strong effects by depolarizing neurons sufficiently to trigger action potentials. Low-intensity TMS seems to mostly stimulate low-threshold inhibitory interneurons, whereas higher intensities excite projection neurons.

TMS pulses can be applied singly, but for therapeutic use, multiple pulses are rapidly applied [repetitive transcranial magnetic stimulation (rTMS)]. When used as an anti-depressant therapy, TMS produces a clinical benefit without the systemic side effects typical with oral medications, has no adverse effects on cognition, and unlike ECT does not induce amnesia or seizures. TMS may be covered when prescribed and supervised by a licensed psychiatrist or neurologist who is trained and knowledgeable in the use.

When effective, TMS can replace antidepressants or switching

DOI: 10.4324/9781003128571-13

antidepressants while treating depression in the brain rather than expose the entire body to antidepressants. It also can prevent the need to utilize more complex pharmaceutical augmentation strategies (e.g., atypical antipsychotic medication), electroconvulsive therapy (ECT), and inpatient hospitalization at later stages of the illness.

Once, I recommended this treatment to a patient with stubborn depression and multiple failed responses to interventions. The patient took this recommendation back to her primary care doctor. He, however, rejected it as quackery. So, this example illustrates the continued disconnect between medical providers and clinicians when it comes to understanding the behavioral health component of a patient's care. One solution is to embed behavioral health components into the primary care practice itself.

This section looks at the way behavioral health can be integrated into primary care. Again, for the purpose of clarity, behavioral health encompasses addiction care.

The argument for incorporating behavioral health into primary care is simple: People are much more likely to visit a primary care facility than a psychiatric health center. Studies also show that people are more willing to enter substance use treatment in a primary care setting compared to specialty addiction treatment centers (Barry, 2016).

Integrating mental healthcare into primary care meets patients where they are. Currently, PCPs diagnose and treat more mental health problems than behavioral health specialists do. About 70% of diagnoses and treatment for mental health issues—including anxiety, mood, and substance use disorders—take place in a primary care setting (Institute for Healthcare Improvement, 2021)

Therefore, medical providers should be rewarded for expanding their capacity and productivity while being reinforced for accepting the identity of a behavioral healthcare provider. This will reduce stigma and enhance team health.

The majority of SSRIs are prescribed in a primary care setting. However, PCPs usually do not have the training to treat these problems adequately. This is evidenced, for example, by the fact that only 10% of patients diagnosed with depression in this setting receive care efficacious enough to achieve remission (Pence, 2012). This is not surprising, since PCPs are not primarily behavioral health providers. It is like asking a brain surgeon to act as a dentist. No one can be an expert in all fields. The way to address this problem is the integration of BHPs into primary care practices. Therefore, medical providers should also have access to resources and be supported by the behavioral health provider communities.

The PCP should have a relationship with a psychiatrist to provide consultation related to initiating medication-assisted treatment for mental health issues. A psychiatric consultant is a key resource for a primary care practice seeking to provide care across the spectrum. Very few primary practices will be able to have a psychiatrist on staff, even if they have behavioral health specialists integrated into their team. But having a psychiatrist who can be called for consultations on matters of diagnosis and medications is essential. Scheduled, weekly consultations allow the PCP to review the progress of patients, while ad hoc phone calls to the psychiatric consultant can provide direction in a timely manner. A consultation while the patient is in the clinic can help the PCP quickly decide whether a referral is necessary, eliminating the need for an additional appointment (Kern & Raney, 2017).

Within a primary care setting, the responsibilities of the behavioral health provider vary according to the level of integration. In a fully integrated setting, the BHP functions as part of a collocated team within primary care. The in-house BHP provides case management along with triage and assessment for both behavioral health and substance use issues. The BHP will consult with the PCP on individual cases, some of which will result in the patient being seen by the BHP for mental health issues. The BHP will also work with the PCP to develop a mental health screening process that will be given to all patients (based on patient populations) in order to identify potential behavioral health issues. Above all, the BHP will work with the PCP and other health providers to develop a single treatment plan that will address the patients' needs in a holistic manner.

This embedded BHP model is ideal. It is not easy, however, to be a BHP in a primary care setting. The BHP must possess extraordinary confidence and skill set. For patients who lack the resources to know or communicate their needs, the BHP provides ego strength. Sometimes people who need BHPs are in a state of feeling beaten down and unimportant. They have been such a burden to their families, employers, and society at large that they do not feel a sense of worth. So, in the initial stages of therapy, it is not uncommon for a patient to rely on the BHP's belief in their compassion for who they are as a human being to take basic steps to protect themselves.

On top of that, in a primary care setting, the BHP must lead the behavioral health needs of the patient—making sure that important behavioral health needs are not being ignored by the rest of the treatment team. The BHP is the lead person who is proficient in promoting engagement, rapid assessment, treatment planning, communicating progress, anticipating barriers, coaching, and developing holistic theories. From initial contact with the care provider team and patient, the BHP must understand the verbal and non-verbal communication being transmitted. They must be vigilant and agile regarding the prioritization of assessments and interventions, as well as the systemic impact of these experiences. They must have an exceptional understanding of the neuro-bio-psycho-social-spiritual interactions within each patient while being fully appraised of the complex social support structures of each individual. They must be strategic in knowing when to act and when to withhold actions. BHPs coordinate the step care process that is measured based on appropriate solutions and then monitored for compliance and outcomes. Although this role may appear briefly in the primary care setting, the BHP is fully aware of the protracted nature of mental health and substance use disorder needs and is prepared for ongoing engagement.

BHPs need to ensure that they are available as much as possible when working within a primary care setting. This requires them to balance scheduling to include appointments, consultations, and free periods. Briefly stepping out of a meeting with a patient for a quick consultation on another patient may be required at times.

Consider these five core functions of the BHP in a primary care setting (Scott & Mendez-Shannon, 2017) which are as follows:

- Patient engagement
- Assessment and triage
- Treatment intervention
- Follow-up and referral coordination
- Data management

Patient engagement is an important aspect of a BHP's role. A good relationship between a therapist and a patient is one of the keys to a successful course of treatment. In a primary care setting, a BHP can take advantage of the trust that already exists between the PCP and the patient. When a patient is transferred to a BHP via a "warm handoff" by a PCP, that relationship already has a head start. Patients who have this relationship are more engaged in both their physical and mental healthcare, which improves patient response to treatment. This is especially true with mental health. One study of health providers indicates that having an integrated BHP onsite increases patients' willingness to follow through since they know that the treatment is located in an environment that is already familiar to them and is convenient (Miller-Matero, 2016).

BHPs also engage in assessment and triage. Assessment is done both directly and indirectly. It occurs directly when a BHP is called to consult on a patient or is given a patient through a warm handoff. It then becomes the responsibility of the BHP to examine the PCP's concerns to see if they warrant further assessment, a diagnosis, further treatment, or even a referral to a mental health specialist. This process indirectly assists the PCP's behavioral health skill development. The BHP can educate PCPs in the interpretation of responses on the forms. It can also lead to the development of a standardized set of screening protocols to be given to clients according to the PCP's patient population.

The BHP also makes decisions concerning the appropriate level of care. Some patients can be treated with continued primary care visits, some will need to be sent to a specialist, and others may require residential treatment. Accurate triage ensures that patients receive the appropriate care in the correct setting. This not only leads to better health outcomes but also contains the costs associated with patients receiving care that is not a fit to their level of need.

Another function of BHPs in a primary care setting is treatment intervention. BHPs in these settings have the benefit of a long-term relationship with patients. They are able to monitor patient progress over time and develop meaningful goals to address issues. By nature, each interaction with a patient will be brief, which means the provider must focus on a particular issue that takes priority over others. Because they will see the patient again in a few months, they have the chance to assess progress. If a goal has been achieved, the BHP can work with the patient to develop another goal that addresses a different problem or a different aspect of the same problem. This has the dual benefit of providing the patient with ownership of their treatment while not overloading them with the idea that all problems need to be addressed at once.

Mental health issues can often seem overwhelming, but breaking the problem into smaller components makes it seem more manageable and gives the patient a sense of hope and self-efficacy for improving their condition. BHPs work with patients to help them manage the emotional aspects of their physical conditions, which can contribute to better somatic health. In tandem with PCPs, they can address behavioral issues associated with healthier living and disease management (Ward, 2016).

Mental health providers also work with patients on follow-up and referral coordination. When a patient is referred to a specialist or program outside the practice, it is necessary for someone in primary care to follow up to make sure the patient has contacted the specialist and kept the appointment. When the referral is to a mental health specialist, the duty of follow-up naturally falls to the BHP.

The BHP also assists patients in overcoming barriers that prevent them from keeping appointments. These can include issues like childcare and transportation that are particularly important in clinics serving poorer areas. The BHP also makes sure all appropriate medical information is sent to the specialist in preparation for the visit.

Finally, the BHP is responsible for data management. In the same way that physicians use EHRs to track somatic health, BHPs can use these same systems to track mental health issues. Comparison of patient measurements over time show areas of progress and issues that continue to need monitoring. The EHR also provides a way to engage in measurement-based care, as it indicates which therapists and which approaches work best, allowing adjustments to be made as needed. BHPs need to keep these records within the primary care setting, allowing reports to be created for regular patient status reviews.

By definition, PCPs are accustomed to working in primary care settings. What is new to them in integrated health is working alongside

BHPs. Learning how to work as a team with BHPs and how to best leverage the expertise of each is key to successful integration. PCPs provide leadership for the team and are sometimes the care coordinators. They assist in the treatment of behavioral health problems by identifying potential issues, both through their interaction with patients and through the use of standardized screening instruments. They can also prescribe and monitor medication used to treat mental illnesses.

PCPs are the main coordinators of care under this model. It is their responsibility to work with other members of the team to develop a treatment plan, then monitor its progress, while making sure that appropriate care is being provided by everyone on the team. They set the order of treatment so that efforts are not being doubled or working at cross purposes. They also serve as the main point of contact for the patients, who have the comfort of knowing that they only need to check with one person when a problem arises. In such cases, the PCP ultimately may not be the one to provide the treatment, but they will direct the patient to the appropriate person. This reduces the complexity of the patient experience and helps them feel more at ease in seeking help.

The PCP also serves as the first line of defense in recognizing and diagnosing mental illness. As noted earlier, about 70% of mental health diagnoses and treatments occur in primary care settings. Early detection increases the likelihood of positive treatment outcomes, and PCPs often have the earliest chance to detect a problem. Working with the BHP to understand the signs of mental illness and using standardized assessment instruments like K-10, GAD-7, and PHQ-9, the PCP can identify signs that would indicate the need for a consultation with or intervention by a BHP.

The final responsibility of PCPs in an integrated primary care setting is the prescription and monitoring of medications that treat mental illnesses. As medical doctors, PCPs have the ability to write prescriptions, which is a systemic intervention itself—unlike most BHPs, who are master's level therapists or doctor's level psychologists. Some PCPs are understandably reluctant to prescribe medications for illnesses they lack the training to diagnose and treat. Others are willing to prescribe initial doses to treat acute cases, but require the patient to see a psychiatrist for any subsequent renewals. This adds a layer of difficulty for patients seeking to manage their medications, as they now must have appointments in multiple facilities to renew a prescription. In an integrated setting, however, the BHP is available for consultation and can help the PCP make better-informed decisions. The process could also be improved through a relationship with a psychiatric consultant.

Achieving integrated health in a primary care setting requires additional staff and facilities. Although the BHP uses the same support staff as the PCP for scheduling and billing, that staff may need to be expanded to absorb a larger workload.

BHPs will also require dedicated assistants and practice space. The number and type of rooms will vary according to the type of services provided. At a minimum, the BHP will need an office. Some BHPs hold sessions in their offices, but others prefer using a room dedicated to that purpose. If the BHP will be holding group sessions, they will need a large enough room and sufficient seating to accommodate the group.

Bringing Primary Care into General Mental Health Settings

When I worked at Lakeview Health, I managed a team of medical providers, including PCPs. They diagnosed a wide variety of medical conditions in that setting.

Having a robust medically informed team allowed for the identification of Gitelman syndrome, which is an inherited kidney disorder with chronically low potassium and magnesium; Lance-Adams syndrome, which is a rare cardiopulmonary resuscitation condition impacting myoclonic jerks/tremors and cerebellar ataxia/unsteadiness; and difficult-to-control insulin-dependent diabetes after pancreatectomy from alcohol pancreatitis. One PCP at Lakeview identified hepatic encephalopathy with alcoholic hepatitis, which caused both high ammonia levels and confusion. The team identified patients with a need for anticoagulation therapy or dialysis. And they routinely diagnosed COPD, asthma, hypertension, sleep apnea, hyperlipidemia, steroid-induced disorders, and diabetes.

These diagnoses tell the powerful story of integrated care in a behavioral health setting. The goals are different from those in a primary care setting but are closely related. In a primary care setting, the goal is the provision of behavioral health services to a population that often does not receive them. In a behavioral health setting, the aim is to increase physical care for a group whose mental illnesses can be barriers to receiving medical treatment. As mentioned earlier, the NIMH reports that people with mental illnesses and substance use disorders have higher rates of chronic somatic illnesses and die earlier than those without such conditions (NIMH, n.d.). Despite their need, this is also a population whose members can be less likely to seek medical attention, which increases numerous risk factors. Patients with serious mental illnesses can also be difficult to treat, as their psychological issues can interfere with their ability to work with their treatment team members.

The role of medical providers in some addiction treatment centers has already been discussed in Chapter 6—Whole Person Care, but this section will address the topic in the broader setting of non-specialized mental health facilities. The primary responsibility of the PCP in such a behavioral health facility is the diagnosis and treatment of physical illnesses among clients who are already utilizing mental health services.

A number of factors can prevent people with serious mental illnesses from availing themselves of medical treatment, and those who do often find their mental disorders hamper their ability to take full advantage of that care. For example, people with anxiety or depression may experience going to see a doctor as being too far outside their comfort zone. Receiving bad news from a doctor may increase their depression or anxiety, so some find it better to avoid knowing. Some may have a general distrust of strangers, including a new doctor. Others may be too mentally ill to care about their physical health, while others lack the intellectual or psychological resources needed to navigate the healthcare system.

Many of these barriers can be overcome in a behavioral health setting. The patients are already at the facility, so getting medical treatment does not require another trip to a different facility. It also means working within a system in which they are already established and which they know how to navigate. Just as in a primary care setting, a warm handoff from a doctor the patient already knows and trusts (the BHP) can overcome the uncertainty of being treated by a new person (the PCP). And for patients who are uncooperative during the exam, a BHP can be present to help the PCP navigate those difficulties. A PCP operating in a behavioral health setting allows patients with serious mental illness to receive more physical healthcare than they otherwise would.

The PCP also works with BHPs to develop a unified treatment plan that incorporates care of both physical and mental health issues. The team-based care model allows care to be coordinated across the spectrum, addressing each need in its proper order. The PCP will attend daily huddles and staffings prior to seeing patients to discuss the clients to be seen that day. They will keep the BHPs up to date on how the physical treatment is progressing and, in turn, receive an update on the behavioral issues of their patients. The huddle/report is also a time for each specialty to consult with the other on questions that arise.

In cases of serious physical illness that need treatment beyond an office visit, PCPs are responsible for making and coordinating referrals. They will refer the patient to the appropriate specialists and help them make an appointment. They are also responsible for the follow-up with the patient to make sure the appointment was kept. The PCP will also receive an update on treatment in order to monitor progress. Just as with a BHP in a primary care setting, the emphasis is on continuing care management instead of episodic visits. Keeping patients with severe mental illness engaged in care is critical to improved health.

Adding medical facilities to a behavioral health setting is a bigger challenge than the other way around. The footprint of a PCP in behavioral health is larger than that of a BHP in primary care. Sufficient staff, rooms, and equipment will need to be added to an existing mental health practice in order to facilitate integrated care. In addition to an office for the PCP, one or more properly equipped medical examination rooms will need to be available. Each must be fully equipped with the standard medical devices and supplies, including an exam table, digital thermometer, sphygmomanometer, otoscope, ophthalmoscope, gloves, swabs, and tongue depressors. A nurse's station and a lab for drawing blood must also be available. For optimal services, the lab must have access to rapid laboratory results.

In terms of staff, the PCP will require nurses and perhaps a case manager, in addition to an administrative staff person.

Trans-organizational Cooperation

The components discussed in this chapter thus far—patients, leadership, and staff—are all internal to the practice. Given the nature and complexity of modern healthcare, however, no one facility can have the resources to treat all issues. Health organizations, therefore, must cultivate a network of resources upon which they can call when the need arises. This section discusses some of the more common resources.

Trans-organizational cooperation involves integrating behavioral and physical healthcare through collaboration between separate organizations. Measured against the SAMHSA levels of integration, this term would encompass Levels 2–4:

- Level 2: Basic collaboration at a distance
- Level 3: Basic collaboration onsite
- Level 4: Close collaboration onsite with some system integration

It is conceivable that close collaboration could occur between organizations that are not collocated (that is, Level 4 or even higher without the onsite and system integration aspects). This level of integration would be difficult to maintain across physical separation. But I believe it is possible.

At lower levels of integration, a primary care clinic may only have an informal relationship with a BHP. In such a situation, the PCP initiates ad hoc consultations, in which the BHP helps PCPs understand and treat mental health issues. The PCP may also refer patients to the BHP, but because studies show that 20–60% of referrals do not show up for their initial appointment, referrals do not always result in treatment (Reust, 1999). Little to no ongoing collaboration takes place, and the BHP does not follow the progress of individual patients. If a patient is referred to a BHP and does follow through, their progress is seldom tracked by the PCP.

For a slightly higher level of integration across organizations, take the example of the relationship between an addiction treatment center and a detox facility. Fully integrated care would require the presence of a medical detox facility, which would allow both steps in the process to be handled at the same facility. This allows behavioral health clinicians to begin developing a relationship with the patient earlier, which leads to greater trust. Clinicians can also start tailoring the course of treatment to the patient's needs before they even complete detox. This will obviously add to the staffing requirements of the center, as doctors and nurses trained in addiction medicine will need to be employed. But the reality is that most addiction treatment centers currently have partnerships with nearby detox facilities instead of handling the detox onsite. Patients only enter the drug and alcohol treatment program once they have completed detox elsewhere. This would qualify as Level 2 integration under the SAMHSA rubric.

For an even higher level of trans-organizational integration, let us go back to Lakeview Health. There I instituted a pain recovery program. We could not call it pain management because we were not going to be providing medications to our patients. They were in substance use recovery, after all. So, we hired a psychiatrist who was also board-certified in pain management. But we could not hire everyone I wanted to have. So, a key part of the integration there was getting a contract with a physical therapist and a physiatrist team, who came in and performed assessments on every patient and worked with patients three days a week. They literally set up their tables and equipment while utilizing our state-of-the-art fitness center which was staffed by full-time exercise physiologists.

We also relied heavily, in general, on partnerships with Mayo Clinic providers. We got all of our providers' privileges at the Mayo Clinic, and they would go over and do grand rounds. In turn, the Mayo Clinic would refer to us whenever they had a need for substance use treatment. The partnership was incredibly valuable. Finally, we had formal relationships with academic institutions in the community where we provided clinical internships and supervision for various professional schools (e.g., psychiatric nurse practitioners, physical therapists, mental health counselors, and social workers.)

No practice can be expected to have experts in all fields. It would be both financially draining and unnecessary. But they do need to have a connection to such specialists for referrals. An integrated care practice must have network resources for any specialty not covered by the facility.

Ideally, this network is explicit, with a relationship developed between the organization and those to whom it wants to send patients. Not only will this provide a smoother experience for all involved, but the relationship between the organization and the specialist can engender trust between the patient and the specialist. Although a warm handoff is not always possible with off-site specialists, patients who know that their PCP is referring them to someone they trust can help them feel more at ease with the referral.

Cooperation between organizations can take several forms, including referral services, contracts, consultation, joint development of treatment plans, reciprocal screening processes, and provider education. Once established, the two systems must continue to sustain their engagement through joint strategic efforts, staff meetings, shared industry discoveries and implementation, and secured privileges in both facilities.

Bidirectional consultation in this model usually takes the form of ad hoc discussions about patients. Physicians consult with behavioral health specialists about mental health issues in their patients. In turn, mental health counselors will contact medical doctors to discuss somatic problems their patients are having. Consultation is usually over the phone or via email, although in cases of collocated practices, face-to-face consultation may take place as well. The impetus for consultation is the need of individual patients. When a patient presents with problems, not in the field of the care provider, a consultation will be requested. The intent is to help the provider make treatment decisions, including whether a referral could be necessary.

Ideally, both PCPs and BHPs will build relationships with organizations in each other's fields. This is most easily done when practices are co-located but can be achieved in separate locations as long as it has the buy-in of the leadership at both practices. The ongoing relationship builds trust between the different providers and makes the consultation process run more smoothly. Such an approach is preferable to providers haphazardly contacting specialists in other fields to get input. The time and effort needed to establish the partnership is repaid by the increase in the quality of care provided, as well as the organizational and professional benefits.

Under this model, each specialty usually develops its own treatment plan for patients, although at Level 4 joint treatment plans may be developed for some clients. But with proper consultation, an informed treatment plan can be designed that addresses both physical and mental health needs, especially for patients that present with low-level issues. Whereas a joint treatment plan would be possible in a fully coordinated medical health home, patients with moderate to severe problems will probably require referral to a specialist. Even within Levels 2–4, PCPs and BHPs are able to track the progress of their patients and encourage follow-through with other providers.

Clinicians should also work to help patients negotiate the resources within the clinic and beyond, connecting them to community resources as varied as housing, nutrition, wellness resources, childcare, and 12-step groups. These community support groups are another facet of the outside resources that a trans-organizationally integrated practice can provide. These groups provide a variety of functions. Some help patients with practical matters, such as housing, child care, and transportation that can be barriers to receiving healthcare. Others are groups that support patient progress. These are especially prominent in addiction treatment, where Alcoholics Anonymous, Al-Anon, and other 12-step organizations provide peer support.

Other organizations provide services, such as in-home therapy, or medical supplies, such as oxygen tanks or CPAP machines. Health homes need to be able to put their patients in touch with these organizations so that healing continues outside the walls of the clinic.

A final way for PCPs and BHPs to integrate healthcare through trans-organizational cooperation takes the form of educational opportunities. It is difficult enough to keep up with advances in one's own field, and staying current on best practices in other areas is almost impossible. But some steps in that direction can be made through seminars and updates provided by other specialties. For example, a BHP could give a talk about screening tools to use for substance use disorders within a collaborating facility. This would be an efficient way of not only informing the entire staff about the use of such instruments but also strengthening the relationship between the two groups. Providers who have met face-to-face are more likely to collaborate in the future. Education also builds trust between practices, as each learns to appreciate the role the other plays in treatment. Inviting respective staff to occupy each other's workspace promotes inclusion and direct discussion as mentalization enhances engagement.

References

Barry, C. L. (2016). Estimating demand for primary care-based treatment for substance and alcohol use disorders. *Addiction, 111*(8), 1376–1384.

Institute for Healthcare Improvement. (2021). *SBAR tool*. Retrieved from Institute for Healthcare Improvement: http://www.ihi.org/resources/Pages/Tools/SBARToolkit.aspx

Kern, J., & Raney, L. (2017). The psychiatric consultant. In L. E. Raney, G. B. Lasky, C. Scott (Eds.), *Integrated care: A guide for effective implementation* (pp. 161–183). Arlington, VA: American Psychiatric Association Publishing.

Miller-Matero, L. R. (2016). Benefits of integrated behavioral health services: The physician perspective. *Families, Systems and Health, 34*(1), 51–55.

NIMH. (n.d.). *Integrated care*. Retrieved from https://www.nimh.nih.gov/health/topics/integrated-care/index.shtml

Pence, B. W. (2012). The depression treatment cascade in primary care: A public health perspective. *Current Psychiatry Reports, 14*(4), 328–335. doi: 10.1007/s11920-012-0274

Reust, C. E. (1999). Keeping or missing the initial behavioral health appointment: A qualitative study of referrals in a primary care setting. *Families, Systems and Health, 17*(4), 399–411. doi: 10.1037/h0089892

Scott, C., & Mendez-Shannon, C. E. (2017). Behavioral health provider essentials. In L. E. Raney, *Integrated care: A guide for effective implementation* (pp. 91–125). Arlington, VA: American Psychiatric Association Publishing.

Ward, M. C. (2016). The role of behavioral health in optimizing care for complex patients in the primary care setting. *Journal General Internal Medicine, 31*(3), 265–267. doi: 10.1007/s11606-015-3499-8

14 The Payoff

If you read this far, you are probably already working in some capacity in the healthcare system. I do not need to tell you about the terrible patient experience that results from the current dysfunction in our system. At various times in your life, you have also been a patient. I do not need to tell you about the powerlessness people often feel when engaging in healthcare.

This powerlessness is much the same that we all felt at the onset of the COVID-19 pandemic. Years after we recover from the pandemic, I hope we never forget how this felt. We should never forget the harmful conspiracies that developed as a result of bad communication.

But it does not have to be this way. At the beginning of my career as a social worker, something of great value was given freely to me: The opportunity to deliver integrated care. And with that, came the opportunity to help people recover from one of the most intractable, destructive, and common disorders. A disorder that does not just destroy bodies—it destroys whole families. A disorder that drains personal wealth and municipal budgets alike.

I was handed the tools to pull people out of this disorder's vice grip and learn to manage it and live. Those early career opportunities have given me extraordinary wealth—in terms of personal impact and satisfaction and, of course, further opportunity. I have not taken this privilege for granted.

I know that most healthcare providers and business leaders are not as lucky as I was. But hopefully, this book has given you the tools as well.

Now you can recognize the significance of the moment you are in. Now you can spot the opportunity that integrated care offers.

Having read this far, you know the complicated path of integrated care's evolution. You know what barriers to expect in implementing it in your own practice. You know how to convince others of integrated care's value. You have a nuanced understanding of the role that leadership and various staff members will play. You know to prioritize communication, and you know the structures and styles of communication to implement. And hopefully, if you are already actively working in healthcare, you have some special tools to use in the setting in which you care for patients.

DOI: 10.4324/9781003128571-14

You know that good technology is essential but not enough. You know that doing the hard work of examining racial and cultural biases—both personal and institutional—is essential but not enough. You know that implementing truly integrated care is an extremely high standard of conduct, but you know that it is worth it.

The addiction crisis and the pandemic make the need for integrated care more imperative than ever. The nature of addiction means it would be best approached in a coordinated fashion even in the absence of a crisis because addiction is both a psychological and physiological condition. Therefore, both behavioral health and medical providers must be a part of prevention, diagnosis, treatment, and aftercare. However, just having all fields involved in treatment is not enough. Communication among all providers must be enabled so that care can be delivered in a coordinated manner.

The call to action for integrated services is driven by data on rising mortality rates with SUDs. This mortality is driven by many etiologies. First are alarming behavioral trends in drug use, overdose, and suicide, as well as continued tobacco use. Second are trends in physical comorbidities—such as cardiovascular diseases, cancer, and infectious disease. And a final contributor are broader societal issues—such as economic factors, social deterioration, deceased marital and employment rates, and suicide (Hser, 2017).

We can turn these etiologies around. But we will have to do it one patient at a time. Integrated care is the answer.

Today, as I travel around the country providing program evaluations, consultation, leadership for treatment providers, and review abstracts on conference committees, I notice more and more healthcare professionals and policymakers understand the importance of integrated care. This has been in the response to the pandemic, which highlighted the need to achieve and maintain physical and behavioral health when faced with complex diseases. The focus shifted to and conversations included Social Determinants of Health (SoDH). It illustrated the importance of early diagnosis of disease states, which improves outcomes when multiple providers work towards the same health goals. This holistic and comprehensive care of mind, body, spirit, emotion, and behavior identifies the individual, not just a disease. Focusing on individuals allows us to fix the cause of the condition, not just alleviate their symptoms.

The pandemic is a tragedy on economic and personal levels. Being in a pandemic has a profound impact on people's mental status. But I am hopeful that these awful trends may help fuel the destigmatization of seeking mental health services—similarly to how the Me Too movement raised awareness of sexual harassment issues. As a result of that movement, I experienced acquaintances and friends who would normally never reveal sexual histories open up about their own victimization.

In a few years, we will just be beginning to see the mental health impacts on the doctors and nurses, the first responders, the people working in public transit systems and food service, and other sectors where the pain was felt. And as we work through it, I am hopeful that it will open up the opportunity for more innovative and inclusive care models.

Through care management and collaboration, integrated care meets people where they are and delivers the services they need. This model of care does not just improve outcomes for patients—it improves the lives of the professionals who serve them. It decreases expenditures, boosts profitability, reduces employee churn, and fuels organic marketing for the organizations where these patients seek care.

Integrated care is the gold standard. No matter how you measure success, implementing this model of care is a good idea. This book is a call to action to healthcare—both business leaders and providers—to not only recognize the opportunity that this model offers but to advance it in their own systems and practices.

Advocacy on behalf of integrated care beyond the organization is also important. This includes not only advocacy by the leadership but also by the staff. Being aware of the barriers to integrated care and sharing how your own group has overcome those barriers is an important part of the process. Promoting integrated care at the community and state level not only leads to greater integration outside the organization but also increases commitment to the model within the organization. In this way, telling your organizations' success story often leads to better self-management of employees and stronger relationships with community members.

Recognizing a major historical change while it is happening is incredibly difficult, especially in healthcare. We have all put on blinders to the seemingly intractable problems that go on every day around us. Why focus on something you cannot change? We have all been reduced to the simplistic survival of an individual struggling with addiction—going to work each day and just providing the best care we feel like we can given the tragic limitations of the structures in which we work.

No more. The IPO is today. Get in early.

And, in a few decades, you will be sitting on a pile of wealth you cannot imagine. That is countless stories of lives you have saved.

With the help, of course, of everyone on your team.

Reference

Hser, Y. J. (2017). High mortality among patients with opioid use disorder in a large healthcare system. *Journal of Addiction Medicine, 11*(4), 315–319.

Index

A.M. Best ratings 91
absenteeism 47
accountable care organizations (ACOs) 118
Accreditation Council for Graduate Medical Education (ACGME) 48–49
addiction: consequences of 4; crisis 20–23, 139; existential crisis and 4; *see also* substance use disorders (SUDs)
addiction treatment: debugging and 1; detoxification 134–135; family programs 52; history of 9–10; models 15–16; primary intervention 54–55; professional 13–16; secondary intervention 54–55; tertiary interventions 55–60
Adverse Childhood Effects (ACE) instrument 53
Affordable Care Act of 2010 39–40
Affordable Care Act of 2014 49
aftercare planners 63
Agency for Healthcare Research and Quality (AHRQ) 23, 44–45, 54, 73, 109, 121
Al-Anon 136
alcohol addiction 22; asylums for 12–13, 14; history 10; mutual aid societies and 12–13; physical damage from 58; professional treatment 13–16; temperance movements and 10–12; *see also* substance use disorders (SUDs)
alcohol consumption 10
Alcoholics Anonymous (AA) 12, 13, 98, 136
American Academy of Family Physicians (AAFP) 121

American Academy of Pediatrics (AAP) 121
American College of Healthcare Executive 101
American College of Physicians (ACP) 34, 68, 96, 121–122
American Osteopathic Association (AOA) 121
American Psychiatric Association (APA) 14
American Society of Addiction Medicine (ASAM) 20, 55
Angie's List 91
anti-mask rallies xii
Anti-Saloon League 11
anxiety 24, 33, 36, 36–39, 46, 47, 127, 57, 81, 83, 133
Assertive Community Treatment (ACT) approach 108
assessment and triage 129
Assessment of the "Leader in Leadership" tool 104
asylums 12–13, 14
auxiliary tasks 101

Back to Bedside 48
barriers to integrated care: buy-in 28–29; communication issues 29; overcoming 27–31; payment barriers 29; systemic hurdles 29–30
behavioral healthcare providers (BHPs) 58, 83, 96, 98, 120; aligning with primary care 2; assessment and triage 129; biopsychosocial and spiritual tactics 30; core functions in primary care setting 129–130; data management 130; decisions on level of care 129–130; family counseling 52; follow-up and referral

coordination 130; patient appointment and visit assistance 130; patient engagement 129; primary care providers in mental health settings 132–134; in primary care settings 126–132; trans-organizational cooperation 134–137; treatment intervention 130; treatment of depression 37
Benbow, S. 18
beneficence 36
biological models 15
Black Lives Matter movement xii
burnout 46–48; absenteeism and 47; costs of 112; incidence of 47; indicators of 46–47; measurement tools 111; prevention programs 111–112; secondary traumatic stress and 46–47
Burnout Measure 111
business case for integrated care 43–49; profitability 44–46; staff 46–49
buy-in 28–29

Cadet, J.L. 20
care coordinators 67–72
care team: communication 74; data sharing 85; families' support 123; patient-centered 20, 44; roles of 2, 48
CareDash 91
carfentanil 22
Caron Treatment Centers 51–52
Caron, R. 52
case managers 60
Centers for Disease Control and Prevention 21, 22–23
42 CFR Part 2 regulations 86, 87
characterological models 15
Child and Adolescent Behavior Assessment (CABA-Y) 84
Chit Chat Farms 51
coaching 74
cocaine 59
cognition 75
collaboration levels 135–136
collaborative care 39, xiv
co-located care 119–120
Commonwealth Fund ratings 91
communication 73–77; active promotion of 74–75; model 109–110; overview 73; promoting by design 75–77; SBAR approach to 76–77; in Six C's model 74; team meetings 76

communication issues 29
communication logs 84
comorbidities 139
Competency Assessment Tool-Mental Health (CAT-MH) 101
comprehensive transitional care 123
conditioning models 15
conflict 74
Consumer Health Ratings 91
consumer rating systems 91
cooperation 74
coordinated care 36–37, 118–124; basic collaboration 119; Four Quadrant Clinical Integration Model 123–124; levels of 118–119; minimal collaboration 119; patient-centered medical homes 121–123
coordination 74
core competencies 100–101
CORE CRT Fidelity Scale 108
cost-effectiveness (CE) 39
counselors 59
COVID-19 pandemic 138, xi–xii
Crisis Resolution Teams (CRTs) 108
Current Procedural Terminology (CPT) code 69, 71

Dartmouth ACT Scale (DACTS) 108
data management 130
data sharing 84–90
Davis, R.W. 17–18
debugging 1
deep brain stimulation (DBS) 126
Denver Health Community Health Worker Program 39–40
Department of Health and Human Services 44
depression 9, 24, 33, 36–37, 47, 49, 57, 126, 133
detox 56, 60–64
detoxification 14, 52, 55–56, 97, 134–135
dipsomania 10
discharge planners 63
disease models 15
Disney 95
drug abuse 58
Drug Enforcement Administration (DEA) 22
DSM-5 16

eating disorders 57
educational models 15

electroconvulsive therapy (ECT) 126–127
electronic health records (EHRs) 20, 29, 43, 57, 81, 86, 89–90
emergency department (ED) 85
empowerment 95–97
engagement 95–97
ethical case for integrated care 32–40; coordinated care as best practice 36–37; increased access 39–40; major factors for integration 34–35; organizational values 35–36; physical health outcomes 38–39; risks for not adopting integration 35
evidence-based practices (EBP) 80–81
existential crisis 4

Family and Medical Leave Act (FMLA) 57
family counselors 52, 61
family support 51–52
Federally Qualified Health Centers (FQHC) 84–85
fentanyl 22
first responders 140
fitness facilities 63
Floyd, G. xii
Fosnacht, A. 84–89, 90
Four Quadrant Clinical Integration Model 123–124
Freudenberger, H. 46

GAD-7 81, 83, 130
Gates, B. 3, 84
gender-specific treatment 59
Gold, M.F. 20
Greenleaf, R. 104, 106
A Guidebook of Professional Practices for Behavioral Health and Primary Care Integration (Cohen) 45

Health Insurance Portability and Accountability Act (HIPAA) 29
healthcare practitioners, burnout 47–48
healthcare specializations 17
HealthGrades ratings 91
heroin 21–22; overdose deaths 22
Hester, R.K. 15
HIV/AIDS 53–54
homebrews 11
huddles 76
hydrocodone 21

hyperalgesia 21

Immunology 59
IMPACT program (Improving Mood—Promoting Access to Collaborative Treatment) 40
inebriate homes 14
Information Blocking Rule 88
Institute for Healthcare Improvement 77
insurance companies 67–72
integrated care: business case for 43–49; collaboration levels 135–136; ethical case for 32–40; fall and rise of 16–20; levels of 118–0; overview 1–8; staff 2; technology for 84–89; terminology xiv
intensive outpatient programs (IOPs) 95
Intermountain Healthcare Mental Health Integration Program 40

Johnson, V. 19
Joint Commission 77, 80
Joint Principles of the Patient-Centered Medical Home 121

Keeley Gold Cure 13
Keeley Institute 13
Kessler 10 (K-10) 83, 130

Lakeview Health 79
Lance-Adam syndrome 132
Lasky, G. 100
leadership 99–114; auxiliary tasks and 101–102; continuous improvement 106–108; core competencies and 100–101; health promotion 110–114; individualized actions 100–102; information collection 106–108; model communication 109–110; overview 99–100; primary responsibilities 100; servant leadership 104–106; ultimate care managers 104–106
Leapfrog ratings 91
learning organizations 80
Lexicon for Behavioral Health and Primary Care Integration 23–24
licensed clinical social workers (LCSWs) 61

Magstim 126

144 *Index*

Maine Health Access Foundation 100
marriage counselors 61
Martha Washingtonians 12
Maslach Burnout Inventory (MBI) model 46, 111
Maslach, C. 46
Masters and Johnson Trauma/Compulsivity Programs 27
Masters, W. 19
Mayo Clinic 112, 135
Mayo Clinic Proceedings 105
Me Too movement 139
measurement-based care (MBC) 79–92; continuous improvement 90–91; data sharing 84–90; definition of 81; evidence-based practices and 80–81; in learning organizations 80; patient metrics 81–82; ratings systems 91; screenings 82–84
medical errors 47
Medicare and Medicaid Services (CMS) star ratings 91
medicine, behavioral health and 30
Microsoft 3, 9
model communication 109–110
Montreal Cognitive Assessment (MoCA) 84
morphine 20
MS Contin 20
multidisciplinary care 2–3, xiv
multidisciplinary teams 58–59
mutual aid societies 12–13
mutual-aid support groups 98

naloxone 23
NAMI ratings 91
National Association of Addiction Treatment Providers (NAATP) 35, 91
National Institute of Mental Health (NIMH) 34, 132
National Survey of Accountable Care Organizations (NSACO) 23, 118
neurologists 17, 126
New Orleans, clean-up of 11
NICELY DONE mnemonic 75
NIDA Modified ASSIST (NM ASSIST) 83
nurse practitioners 57, 60
nurses 18, 59, 60; in addiction treatment centers 135; burnout 47; in Four Quadrant model 124; job satisfaction 106, 114; mental health impacts on 140

obsessive–compulsive disorder (OCD) 57
Office of the National Coordinator 88
Olinde, A. 17
Open Minds 90
opioid use disorder (OUD) 85
opioid-induced bowel dysfunction 59
opioids: addiction 21; addiction crisis 20–23, 58; as analgesics 20–21; hyperalgesia.and 21; immune deficiency and 59; prescriptions 21; treatment of overdoses 23
opium 14
organizational strategies 71–72
organizational values 35–36
overdose: deaths 5, 49; heroin 22; opioid 23, 85
oxycodone 20–21
OxyContin 20–21

pain recovery specialists 58
pass down report 84
patient advocacy 69
patient engagement 103, 129
patient experience 94–98; empowerment 95–97; engagement 95–97; transitional care 97–98
Patient Health Questionnaire 9 (PHQ-9) 81, 83, 130
patient metrics 81–82
patient relationship management (PRM) 95
patient-centered medical homes 121–123
payment barriers 29
person-centered peer workers 63–64
Petty, T. 22
Pevsner, V. 27, 79
physiatrists 58
physical health outcomes 38–39
physical therapists 28, 58, 60, 62, 135
physician assistants 57, 59, 60
physicians: and barriers to integrated care 30; burnout in 46–48, 111–112; communication with management 110; emergency 86; financial incentives 110; in integrated care 18, 30, 33; resiliency programs 112; structural bonds 110; and systemic

pay barriers 68; treatment of opioid overdoses 23; use of codes 69; use of electronic health records 130
Pine Grove Behavioral Health and Addiction Services 27
PIP items 102–103, 107
Polles, A. 28
post-acute withdrawal syndrome (PAWS) 56, 60
post-traumatic stress disorder (PTSD) 36, 57, 83
Practice Integration Profile tool 24
Pratt, J.P. 18
primary care providers (PCPs) 43, 58, 83, 98, 120; aligning with behavioral health care 2; in general mental health settings 132–134; in integrated care 48; integration of behavioral healthcare providers into 127–132; risk assessment 53; role as team leader 28–29; screening by 36; trans-organizational cooperation 134–137; treatment of mental health problems 127
primary intervention 54–55
Prince (musician) 22
Professional Enhancement Program 27
profitability 44–46
Prohibition 11, 15
Project TrEAT (Trial for Early Alcohol Treatment) 45
psychiatric care, one-dimensional 9
psychiatric nurse practitioners 60
psychiatrists 9, 17–18, 54–55, 57–58, 60, 86, 126, 127, 127–128, 131, 135
psychoanalysis 2, 15
psychologists 18, 46–47, 55, 60, 60–61, 111, 131
PTSD Checklist (PCL-5) 81, 83
public health model 15

RateMD 91
ratings systems 91
recovery peers/coaches 63–64
recovery-oriented peer workers 63
recovery-oriented system of care (ROSC) 63
registries 84
relationship-focused peer workers 64
repetitive transcranial magnetic stimulation (rTMS) 126
resiliency programs 112
return on investment (ROI) 39, 45–46

Ritz-Carlton Hotel 95
River Oaks Hospital 17–18; Trauma Program 18–19
run-time error 1
Rush, B. 14

Screening, Brief Intervention, and Referral to Treatment (SBIRT) 37, 40, 54
screenings 82–84
Sear, M.L. 18
secondary intervention 54–55
secondary traumatic stress (STS) 46–47
selective serotonin reuptake inhibitors (SSRIs) 127
sensory overload 94
serious mental illness (SMI) 43
Serpa, R. 104
servant leadership 104
sexual disorders 18–19, 82
sexual trauma 18–19
Shatterproof ratings 91
Six C's model 74
smallpox 53
Smith, R. 13
Social Determinants of Health (SoDH) 139
sociocultural model 15
Sorte, B. 51
Sorum, W.S. 17
Southwest Airlines 95
specialists 17
staff: burnout 46–48; gaps in staffing 102; mission and vision 101–102
Staff Burnout Scale for Health Professionals 111
staff meetings 76
Stocks, J.A. 17
strong teams 102
Substance Abuse and Mental Health Services Administration (SAMHSA) 37, 81, 89, 118–119; health promotion 111; levels of integration 135
Substance Abuse and Mental Health Services Administration and the Health Resources and Services Administration (SAMHSA-HRSA) 101
substance use disorders (SUDs) 4, 62–63; admissions 68; DSM-5 classification 16; healthcare workers 47, 49, 51; history 10; immune

deficiency and 60; mortality 139; physical damage from 59–60; professional treatment 13–16; severity specifiers 16; treatment 52
suicide 23, 43, 46, 49, 87, 139
systems models 15

team meetings 76
technology 84–89
telehealth 30
temperance movements 10–12
tertiary intervention 55–58
Tilghman, N. 84–89, 90
transcranial magnetic stimulation (TMS) 126
transitional care 97–98
trans-organizational cooperation 134–137
trauma-informed peer workers 64
treatment intervention 130
Treatment Placement Criteria 91
triage 129, 130
Trusted Exchange Framework and Common Agreement 88
turnover 47
12-step organizations 13, 136

University of California, Los Angeles (UCLA) 113

value on investment (VOI) 68
Vicodin 21
Virginia Commonwealth University (VCU) Medical Center 113
vitals.com 91
voluntary peer workers 64

Washingtonians 12–13
Weisler, J. 18
WHO ratings 91
whole person care 2, 51–65, xiv; primary intervention 54–55; secondary intervention 54–55; tertiary intervention 55–58
whole-person care xiv
Wilson, W.G. 13
withdrawal symptoms 14, 56
Women's Christian Temperance Union (WCTU) 11–12
workflow items 102
workplace screening times 103

Yelp 91

ZocDoc 91
Zulresso 37

Printed in the United States
by Baker & Taylor Publisher Services